LUNA KYUNG & AHNJI

그림으로 만나는 한식

KOREAN CUISINE
AN ILLUSTRATED GUIDE

WRITTEN BY LUNA KYUNG
ILLUSTRATED BY AHNJI

T0346757

FIREFLY BOOKS

TABLE OF CONTENTS

Dough and noodles..........67

Signature and party dishes....................73

Cooking by category.......91

Desserts and drinks.....115

Index.........................126

All the recipes in this book serve 4 people.

한국의 요리

KOREAN FOOD

For Koreans, son-mat is literally translated as "hand taste." It's an expression that is very dear to Koreans and that describes the taste of a well-made dish. It's a way of recognizing that a good dish has all the trademarks of its cook, like a signature. This approach demonstrates the importance between social connections and sharing that is linked with Korean food.

If Korean society is characterized by its hyperactivity, its food provides a welcome break from this culture of speed and efficiency. There is a natural flow and tradition which is comforting. Dining in restaurants is a spiritual experience, bringing guests closer to nature, their social lives and the promise of a peaceful interlude.

MEAL COMPOSITION

In Korea, all dishes are served at the same time; you alternate between eating the rice, soup and side dishes.

가족식사

*Gajok-siksa*가족식사, a home-classic, is made of a *bap*, a bowl of rice, a *guk*, a soup, and *banchan*, as well as a variety of smaller bite-size foods. *Kimchi* is included in most dishes and there are many different types. A main dish is made from either fish or meat. Generally speaking, vegetables make up two thirds of the meal. Dessert culture doesn't exist in Korea and fruit is often provided at the end of meals, although nowadays, younger generations are eating more sweet treats.

Breakfast

Korean breakfasts are almost as filling as lunch.

They include soybean rice, a seaweed soup with beef, cabbage *kimchi*, egg rolls, zucchini *namul*, stir fried anchovies and sweet peppers, and fruit.

아침

Lunch

Doenjang stew, white rice, radish *kimchi*, pickled garlic or *jangajji*, grilled fish, spinach *namul*, preserved tofu, seaweed chips, etc.

Many people eat their breakfast outside, in a cafeteria at school or at work. You'll easily find restaurants offering *baekban*, a "home-style" menu (rice, soup and *banchan*).

점심

Dinner

Multigrain rice, soybean sprout soup, cabbage *kimchi*, water *kimchi*, *bulgogi*, lettuce and perilla leaves, different types of *jang* (*gochujang* and *ssamjang*), scallion salad, preserved lotus root and mushroom *namul* are dishes that make up a typical Korean menu.

Dinner is often eaten as a family, even if the whole family is not always there at the same time due to both parents working and children attending private classes until late evening, especially in cities.

저녁

REGIONAL SPECIALTIES

한국의 지역 특산품

Due to Korea's location on the peninsula, seafood is used as often as livestock. Additionally, as mountains cover an area measuring roughly 136,702 m² (220,000 km), or about 70% of the country, there is a rich variety of mountain and forest produce. The country has been divided into South Korea and North Korea since 1953. Although they share the same culinary heritage, South Korean food has progressed much more due to its connection with the rest of the world.

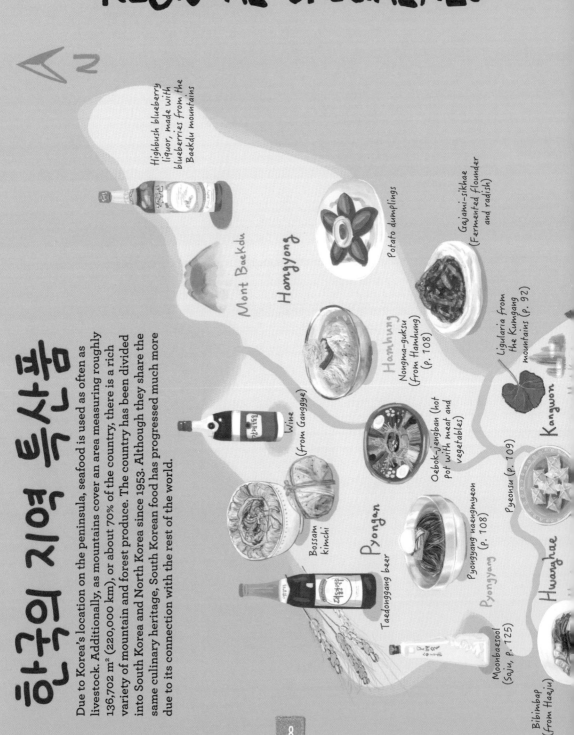

N

Highbush blueberry liquor, made with blueberries from the Baekdu mountains

Mont Baekdu

Hamgyong

Potato dumplings

Gajiami-sikhae (Fermented flounder and radish)

Hamhung
Nongma-guksu (from Hamhung) (p. 108)

Ligularia from the Kumgang mountains (p. 92)

Wine (from Ganggye)

Oebok-jengban (hot pot with meat and vegetables)

Kangwon

Bossam kimchi

Pyongan

Pyongyang naengmyeon (p. 108)

Pyeonsu (p. 109)

Pyongyang

Taedonggang beer

Huanghae

Moonbaesool (Soju, p. 125)

Bibimbap (from Haeju)

Shrimp

Squid

Crab

Seaweed rice roll
with squid (Chungmu)

Potato liquor
(from Pyeongchang)

Pine mushrooms

Andong soju
(p. 56)

Chili pepper
(from Yeonyang)

Seaweed
miyeok guk

Gangwon

Gangneung

Pyeongchang

Andong

Yeonyang

Busan

Acorn jelly
(p. 45)

Sesame

Omija berries
(from Mungyeong)

GyeongSang

Garlic

Eonyang

Jujube

Grapes

ChungCheong

Samgyetang (p. 77)

Bibimbap
(from Jeonju)

Bulgogi
(from Eonyang)

Yuja (yuzu)

Gim, seaweed
sheets

Anchovies

Gyeonggi

Suwon

Seoul
(p. 79)

Ginseng
(from Geumsan)

Jeonju

Jeolla

Pears

Mulhoe (p. 95)

Black pork

Galbi, grilled beef short
ribs (from Suwon)

Azalea flower
liquor

Instant fermented
soy (p. 57)

Oysters

Gaejang
(p. 88)

Gochujang (p. 56)
(from Sunchang)

Sunchang

Fermented
shrimp

Field gromwell
liquor

Seoguipo

Jeju

Clementines
(from Seoguipo)

Bingtteok: thin buckwheat
pancakes with radish

Horse-shaped
cookie

Millet
liquor

THE 5 COLOR PHILOSOPHY

One of the oldest philosophical concepts, Taoism, where the main idea is to lead a "balanced life," has deeply influenced Korean culture. The oheng theory, the five elements of nature, is demonstrated by the variety of colors found in dishes, obangsaek: black (water), blue (wood), white (metal), yellow (earth), red (fire). Green replaces blue in the majority of dishes.

It's *gomyeong* 고명, the finishing touches and decorative elements, that provide these colors in dishes: for example, egg whites, egg yolks, the black in black mushrooms, the red in chilis or dried jujube, the green in celery or scallions.

미나리강회   Minari-ganghoe, bite-size pieces of water celery.

오방색

The five colors, obangsaek.

Obangsaek is a way of embellishing meals, the "cherry on the cake."

Bibimbap is an excellent example. Decorative elements vary and provide plenty of color.

GOMYEONG 고명

Precise cutting is needed to create these decorative elements. The most common shapes to make are thin, matchstick strips, circular disks, diamonds, or they are chopped into small pieces.

Popular foods

Green: ginkgo fruit, *minari* (water celery), zucchini and cucumber skins, scallions.
Yellow: egg yolk, squash, pine pollen, gardenia fruits.
White: egg whites, pine nuts, raw chestnuts, pears, white sesame.
Black: mushrooms, seaweed, dried fern sprouts, black sesame, meat.
Red: chilis, dried jujube, cockscomb (flower), carrots, shrimp.

Examples of gomyeong shapes

달걀 지단

Dalgyal-jidan, strips or diamond-shaped egg whites and egg yolk

Cook the egg yolks and whites separately in a lightly oiled frying pan, over low heat, without browning. Cut the egg into 3 mm wide strips or in diamonds with a width around ¾ of an inch (2 cm).

RULES ON ETIQUETTE

식사 예절

In Korean Confucian tradition, etiquette imposes strict rules on table manners, especially for relationships between younger and older people, descendants and ancestors, as well as between men and women. Men were served their food at individual tables, while women, with the exception of aristocrats, ate their meals with the children. Starting in the middle of the 20th century, post-war national campaigns on economic restrictions brought about new customs: one table for the whole family and standardized sizes of stainless steel dishes with precise dimensions (to save rice). Koreans have only recently been freed from these restrictions.

GOOD MANNERS

Etiquette around your elders

Wait for older people at the table to start or for their permission to start eating.

Only leave the table with their permission.

Serve and take any alcoholic drinks with two hands and bow the head slightly in acknowledgement or give thanks for the drink.

How to correctly hold your chopsticks, jeotgalak.

젓 가락

고맙습니다.
(Thank you)

- Use a spoon for rice and soup, and chopsticks for smaller foods.
- Put the chopsticks down when using the spoon, and vice-versa.
- The spoon should be placed to the left of the chopsticks.

The first spoonful of rice should not be taken from the center, but from around the edges.

Eat while sitting upright.

WHAT NOT TO DO

- Blow on hot food to cool it down, you have to wait until it reaches a good temperature.
- Blow you nose or burp.
- Top up an alcoholic drink before you have finished it.
- Move the cutlery.

Poke around the rice with your cutlery, except when offering food to ancestors.

Hold your spoon and chopsticks at the same time.

Lift your bowl or plate off of the table (like in China or Japan where you would eat with the bowl of rice in your hand and not on the table).

TABLEWARE AND UTENSILS

In Korean history, pottery and metalwork techniques were extremely desirable and a rich and diverse range of table art was created; the beauty of white porcelain or greenish gray celadon is renowned amongst experts.

TABLEWARE, CUTLERY 식기

Dinnerware

도자기

Porcelain: suitable for all seasons.

수저

Sudgalag, jeotgalak, spoons and chopsticks: they are always placed together. Korea is the only country that uses metal chopsticks.

칠기

Lacquer: most commonly used by Buddhist monks.

방짜유기

Bangjja-yugi, copper-tin alloys: winter tableware, it holds heat well.

다구

Dagu, tea service

대접

Stainless steel *daejeop*, large bowl for noodles or noodle soup.

소반

Soban, lacquered coffee table.

뚝배기

Ttukbaegi, clay pot, for stews.

돌솥

Dolsot, a stone bowl for *bibimbap*.

UTENSILS AND EQUIPMENT

옹기

Onggi, clay dishes: Due to the clay and varnish used to make them, these dishes "let the contents breathe," making them perfect for fermented foods.

전골냄비

Large saucepan: used for hot pots.

Tongs and scissors: for cutting meat and more springy noodles.

절구

Stone pestle: perfect for crushing garlic.

불고기 불판

Bulgogi-bulpan, specific *bulgogi* grill.

가스버너

Portable gas stove: to cook grilled meats and hot pots at the table.

석쇠

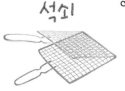

Grilling basket: for grilling seaweed sheets, meat and fish.

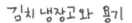

채반

Chaeban: drying rack.

김치 냉장고와 용기

Kimchi-nengjango, kimchi "cave": refrigerators and boxes specifically for *kimchi,* refrigerators replicate the ideal temperature for *kimchi* fermentation.

Containers: for fermentation.

STAPLE PRODUCTS

Here are the most frequently used products.

배추

Baechu, pe-tsaï cabbage (Napa cabbage): essential for making *kimchi*.

무　열무

Mu, daikon radish: has a more subtle flavor than black radish, and firmer than pink radish, one of the most commonly used vegetables.

콩나물

Kongnamul, soybean sprout most popular after the vegetables used in *kimchi*. They can be used in soups or salads, both raw and cooked

미나리

Minari, water celery: aromatic vegetable used in fish soups. It can also be used to make a kind of string to prepare a variety of items (parcels, bouquets, etc.).

쑥

Ssuk, mugwort: aromatic herb that acts as a green coloring in both savory and sweet dishes.

깻잎

Ketnip, perilla leaves: very aromatic, they are often enjoyed with grilled meats

마늘　파

Maneul, garlic, and *pa*, scallions: these are the most commonly used types of seasoning in Korean cooking. They can be found in almost everything, with the exception of Buddhist food.

생강

Sengang, ginger: this winter spice is used in infusions or syrups, but also in *kimchi*.

고추

Gochu, made from fresh red or green chilis.

실고추　고춧가루

Gochugaru, dried red chili flakes, *silgochu*, dried chili 'threads': chili the most recently introduced spice Korea. Having said this, it can be fo in many Korean dishes, in particul *baechu kimchi*, the most popular typ *kimchi*.

멸치

Myeolchi, dried anchovies: for broths or confits.

김

Gim, dried red seaweed sheets (nori): they can be eaten grilled or raw with rice.

다시마

Dashima, brown seaweed (kombu): for broths or *ssam*.

미역

Miyeok, tender brown seaweed: it is used both raw and cooked in soups and salads.

표고버섯

Pyogo-beoseot, shiitake mushrooms: very fragrant, they are cooked with meat or in broths.

깨

Kkhae, black and white sesame seeds, toasted: they provide a nutty flavor and give dishes a decorative touch.

잣

Jat, pine nuts: as kernels, a dry powder or in sauces, they provide a creamy flavor.

대추

aechu, dried jujube: 's almost apple-like avor brings a sweet-ss to both savory and sweet dishes.

은행

Eunhaeng, ginkgo seeds: they are eaten either grilled or crushed, but they are also used to garnish some dishes.

감

Gam, persimmon: made with pears and apples, two of the three most popular Korean fruits. They are often used in *kimchi*.

배

Bae, Asian pears: crisp and more refreshing than French pears.

석류

Seokryou, pomegranate: used in soft drinks and some types of *kimchi*.

유자

Yuja, yuzu: it is used to make some types of *kimchi* and some sauces, for both savory and sweet dishes.

오미자

Omija, the five flavor berry: these are dried and used in sweet dishes.

CONDIMENTS AND SAUCES

Most condiments come from the salt fermentation process, and often replace it in recipes. You can tell the difference between them depending on the way they have been made, in a traditional way or mass-produced. The difference between them not only depends on their quality, but also on the type of microorganisms used in the fermentation process. For example, the taste of traditionally made soy sauce is completely different than mass-produced soy sauce. Traditionally-made condiments with a strong flavor are used for traditional cooking.

CONDIMENTS 양념

재래 된장

Jerae-doenjang: traditional fermented soybean paste.

재래 간장

Jerae-ganjang: traditional soy sauce, and *cheong-jang* is the unaged version (short-term maturation period).

새우젓 / 액젓

Saeujeot, fermented shrimp, and *aek-jeot,* fish sauce: a powerful flavor enhancer.

고추장

Gochujang: traditional fermented soybean paste with chili.

참기름 / 들기름

Cham-gileum and *deul-gileum:* toasted sesame an⬤ perilla oil, the mos⬤ popular aromatic oi⬤ They give Korean fo⬤ its characteristic sm⬤

된장

Mass-produced *doenjang*

간장

Mass-produced *ganjang*

고추장

Mass-produced *gochujang*

매실청

Maesil-cheong: plum syrup for savory dishes.

식초

Sikcho: rice vinegar.

조청

Jo-cheong: rice syrup u⬤ in sweet dish⬤

SAUCES 양념장

Mix all of these ingredients together.

양념간장

Yangnyeom-ganjang, seasoned soy sauce

For *bibimbap* and raw tofu dishes.
- 5 tbsp (75 ml) of soy sauce
- 1 tbsp (15 ml) of honey
- 1 tbsp (15 ml) of toasted sesame oil
- 2 tsp (10 ml) of chopped scallions
- 1 tsp (5 ml) of crushed garlic

양념고추장

Yangnyeom-gochujang, seasoned gochujang

For *bibimbap*.
- ¼ cup (80 g) of *gochujang*
- 2 tbsp (30 ml) of water
- 1 tbsp (15 ml) of sugar
- 1 tbsp (15 ml) of toasted sesame oil
- 2 tsp (10 ml) of soy sauce

삼장

Ssam-jang

For grilled, raw or marinated meats, and *ssam*.
- 5 tbsp (75 ml) of *doenjang*
- 2 ½ tbsp (37.5 ml) of *gochujang*
- 1 tbsp (15 ml) of sesame oil
- 1 tbsp (15 ml) of water
- ½ tbsp (7.5 ml) of sugar
- 2 tsp (10 ml) of crushed toasted sesame seeds
- 1 tsp (5 ml) of chopped garlic

기름장

Gileum-jang, salty sesame oil

For plain grilled meats (not marinated) and grilled mushrooms.
- 1 tbsp (15 ml) of fleur de sel (or sea salt)
- 1 tbsp (15 ml) of sesame oil
- Pepper

초간장

Cho-ganjang, vinegar soy sauce

For fried foods and dumplings.
- Just under ¼ cup (50 ml) of soy sauce
- Just under ¼ cup (50 ml) of rice vinegar

초고추장

Cho-gochujang, vinegar gochujang sauce

For raw fish or seafood dishes.
- 3 tbsp (45 ml) of *gochujang*
- 3 tbsp (45 ml) of rice vinegar
- 1 ½ tbsp (22.5 ml) of sugar
- 1 tbsp (15 ml) of water

강된장

Gang-doenjang, fermented soybean paste with vegetables

For *ssam* and rice.
- Finely chop 8 shiitake mushrooms, 1 zucchini, 1 onion, 4 green chilis, 9 cloves of garlic.
- Sweat the vegetables with 2 tbsp (30 ml) of perilla oil, then add 2 tbsp (30 ml) of *doenjang*, 2 tbsp (30 ml) of *gochujang*, 2 tbsp (30 ml) of honey and ⅓ cup (80 ml) of water.
- Cook the ingredients down until they are very tender.

겨자장

Gyeoja-jang, sweet mustard dressing

For salads.
- Just over ¼ cup (70 g) of apple or pear purée
- 6 tbsp (90 ml) of rice vinegar
- 2 tbsp (30 ml) of pine nut powder
- 1 tbsp (15 ml) of honey
- 3 tsp (15 ml) of mustard
- Salt

맛있는 의성어, 의태어
KOREAN COOKING TERMS

The Korean language has a wide variety of adjectives and words used to describe informal and sensory qualities. In the world of cooking, there are many onomatopoeias and interjections which convey taste, texture and emotion.

Seasoning

Ming-ming: lacks salt, and therefore, flavor (stronger than *seum-seum*).

Seum-seum: a slight lack of salt which gives a blandness to food, allowing you to better taste the "natural" flavor of the ingredients (this is the famous notion of "blandness" in Asian culture, for example, the taste of rice without salt, bland but rich in subtle flavors).

Sam-sam: perfectly salted.

Jjap-jjal: a touch too salty, but still enjoyable.

Textures

Assak-assak: the crunch of wet and light foods (cucumber, salad leaves...).

Ageak-ageak: the crunch of wet and firmer foods (thicker and crunchier vegetables like carrots).

Ba-ssak-ba-ssak: crisp, light, pleasant, crumbles into small pieces (like a cookie that has just been taken out the oven).

Phou-seok-phou-seok: a loose crumbling (like dry bread being turned into bread crumbs).

Go-sseul-go-sseul: used to talk about the cooking of short-grain rice, cooked al-dente, without too much moisture weighing it down.

Phou-sseul-phou-sseul: the texture of long-grain rice, low-moisture and not too sticky.

Mal-lang: pleasantly soft, springy (like freshly baked bread).

Moul-leong: soft, not necessarily in a pleasant way, mushy vegetables (like an overripe peach).

Tchol-guit: soft, very springy rice cakes, pleasant to chew.

Gil-guit: rubbery, tougher meats or fibrous vegetables.

Types

CUTTING – *Song-song*: very thin slices (finely chopped scallions).

Sung-sung: thick slices (chopping a leek into large pieces).

Sung-deong-sung-deong: cut 'soft' products into large pieces (cutting meat for stews).

COOKING – *Bo-geul-bo-geul*: gently boiling, more than a simmer.

Bou-geul-bou-geul: vigorously boiling with large bubbles.

Ji-geul-ji-geul: sizzling oil, a thin layer of oil in a frying pan.

STEAM – *Mo-lak-mo-lak*: a small amount of steam released quickly but steadily (hot rice being taken out of the cooker).

Mou-leok-mou-leok: a lot of steam released vigorously from a large sauce pan or casserole dish.

Smells and actions

Pol-pol: a slight smell — quite pleasant — that grows, but is not too overpowering (subtle smell of toast).

Poul-poul: a smell — quite unpleasant and strong — that grows quickly (rotten smell).

Souhl-souhl: vigorous, clean and quick release of the contents through a wide opening.

Sohl-sohl: slow and light sprinkling of a granular product (careful sprinkling of salt).

ji-geul - ji-geul

지글지글

gil-guit

질깃

tchol-guit

쫄깃

soung-soung

숭숭

bo-geul, bo-geul

오글오글

song-song

송송

sung, deong, sung, deong

숭덩숭덩

Mou-leok-Mou-leok

무럭무럭

bou-geul-bou-geul

부글 부글

mo-lak-mo-lak

모락모락

21

TRADITIONAL MARKETS

One of the defining characteristics of Korea is the coexistence of the ultra-modern and the traditional. Despite the omnipresence of modern malls, traditional markets are still very popular. People love the warmth of a human touch: sellers with big personalities, bulk sales, negotiable prices, etc. The boutiques and stalls on wheels offering candy are a must! There are plenty of markets even in Seoul, Namdaemun-sijang and Gwangjang-sijang to name a couple. Some are dedicated to herbal medicine, Gyeongdong-sijang, or seafood, Noryangjin-susansijang.

식당 IN RESTAURANTS

In Korea, restaurants are often specialized in one area: grilling, tofu, seafood, etc. Bars also offer a variety of dishes to eat. More often than not, restaurants are places that you go to specifically to eat, and not to socialize, with an adjoining outdoor space like in France. So, you would usually eat as a group in a private area, especially at fancy restaurants.

고깃집

Grill restaurants have tables with built-in stoves and removable chimneys. Guests cook their own meat, but the servers can intervene if needed.

POCHA 포차

Ding~dong
On restaurants tables, you
will often find a call button
to alert staff that assistance
is needed. If the person does
not bring you any cutlery,
look under the table, you'll
find it in a drawer.

Pocha are restaurants on wheels found in urban areas. Initially simple and cheap, they've become very fashionable and popular among young people.

In traditional Korean restaurants, you would have sat cross-legged on the floor or on chairs.

Some pochas do not move, but have kept
their traditional style. Here, alcohol,
snacks and "bunsik" dishes are offered
(p. 67).

배달 문화 KOREA, A TAKE-OUT PARADISE

Korean society is characterized by its energy and desire for success; people spend a lot of time at work. To keep up with the ultra-fast pace, the daily commodity services offered are optimized, especially all food delivery services.

Having a picnic by the river Hangang in Seoul.

Ordering ready-made meal boxes is very common, and consumers demand the highest quality. They can be found in stores open 24 hours a day or they can be delivered.

Food can be delivered quickly to anywhere, even outdoor areas with no fixed address. The most popular dish is fried chicken.

Food delivery service leaflets

편의점 도시락
Meal boxes

WORK AND SERVICES AVAILABLE

In Seoul and other large towns and cities, a lot of students and professionals live alone, far from their families. Ready-to-eat dishes can be found everywhere.

Ready-to-eat kimchi

Chapaguri recipe

Empty 1 packet of *neoguri* into 1 quart (liter) of boiling water, then, after 3 minutes, add 1 packet of *chapagheti*. When they are cooked, drain the water, but set just under ½ a cup (100 ml) to the side. Lastly, mix in the seasoning. Pan-fry the beef, season with soy sauce and pepper, and add to the noodles.

Chapaguri (ram-don)
Chapaguri is a very popular snack made from instant noodles, originally created by young people, but now enjoyed by all generations. It became well-known internationally thanks to the movie Parasite.

Delis

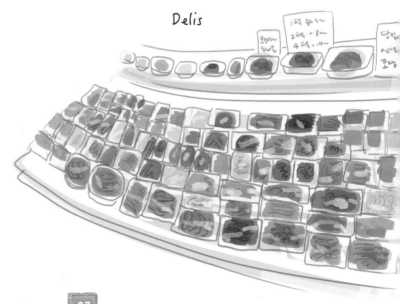

반찬 가게

In households where both parents work, delis offer "home-made" banchan. Using ready-made kimchi is also becoming more and more popular.

집밥

EVERYDAY DISHES

Unlike the usual "appetizer-entree-dessert" meal order, bansang is a prepared table offering everything at the same time.

Originally, this type of meal always included rice, soup, a variety of three, five, seven, nine or twelve different smaller plates (banchan), sauces and kimchi (staple condiments).

Nowadays, this model is rarely followed, but a typical family meal still includes a bowl of rice, soup, banchan and, of course, kimchi.

밥 RICE AND GRAINS

Bap 밥, rice, is like the background in a coloring book. All the flavors and aromas are placed on this white background which brings everything together, allowing all the flavors to mix. Rice is characterized by its simplicity and its subtle presence, and yet a meal without rice is not a proper meal for a Korean. Only one type of rice, the short-grained Japonica variety, is used in Korean recipes. Its texture is soft, springy and slightly sticky. It's from the same variety as sticky rice.

A bowl of white rice on a soban, traditional table.

COOKING RICE: STEP BY STEP

1 Rinse 2 cups (450 g) of short-grain rice 5 times, agitate it by mixing it vigorously, then let it soak in 1 quart (liter) of water for 10 minutes and drain it well. Put it in a saucepan, pour in enough water so that it reaches roughly halfway up your hand and cover.

2 Bring it to the boil over high heat, then turn the heat down to low. Let it cook until all the water has been absorbed, turn the stove off and let it rest for 5 minutes, keeping it covered.

3 Before serving it in individual bowls, fluff the rice using a wet spatula.

4 You can use this recipe for sticky rice by reducing the amount of water by 10%.

Three types of rice

5-grain rice

In addition to the classic ingredients such as rice, sticky rice, kidney beans, millet, soybeans, you can add chestnuts, jujube and ginkgo fruit. This rice is eaten on the evening of the first full moon of the year, with preserved vegetables harvested the year before.

Soybean sprout rice

It is cooked with soybean sprouts and served with seasoned soy sauce (see p. 19).

Black soybean rice

You need to soak large pulses like soybeans in advance, which should usually be done overnight. Save the water they have been soaking in for cooking, as it will now be rich in antioxidants. Soybeans, high in protein, balance out the high carbohydrate content of the rice.

JUK, RICE PORRIDGE

Juk can be translated as "porridge" or "ground rice soup." This dish might be very simple, as it's simply made of rice and water, but it is also complex, as it requires meticulous care (straining, mixing, etc.).

JUK 죽

Jatjuk, with pine nuts

Hobakjuk, with pumpkin and sticky rice balls

Hinjuk, pure rice porridge

Heukimjajuk, with black sesame

Jeonbokjuk, with abalone

This dish has a rich, umami flavor. Either the muscles on their own, or their intestines too, are used to add a hint of iodine.

Hinjuk

1. Let just under 1 cup (200 g) of washed rice in 1.5 quarts (liters) of water soak for 2 hours.

2. Cook this over high heat. Once it is boiling, reduce the heat so that it is very low and continue cooking, stirring regularly until the rice is tender.

3. Serve with seasoned soy sauce, toasted sesame oil and toasted sesame seeds.

Heukimjajuk

1. Soak ¾ cup (160 g) of washed rice in just under 2 ½ cups (600 ml) of water for 2 hours.

2. Wash about ⅔ cup (80 g) of black sesame and pat them dry. Toast them on a medium heat for 10 minutes in a frying pan, stirring continuously during this time. Remove them from the pan and keep them on a plate until you smell a toasted nuttiness.

3. Mix the sesame carefully with 1 ½ cups (350 ml) of water. Set this to the side. Mix the drained rice with just over ¾ cups (200 ml) of water.

4. Add just under 4 cups (900 ml) of water and the rice to a saucepan. Cook the rice over high heat while stirring; once it is boiling, turn the heat down to low and let it cook with the lid on for 20 minutes, stirring often. Add the sesame and continue to cook for a few more minutes. Season with salt (optional). Garnish with pine nuts and dried jujube. Serve hot.

SSAM, SALAD RICE PARCELS

쌈밥

Ssambap, ssam dishes

Recipe: ssam dishes

1 Place a variety of salad leaves, sauces, *ssam-jang*, seasoned *gochu-jang* and *gang-doenjang* (see p. 19), garlic and fresh chopped chilis, *banchan* of your choice and 4 bowls of rice on the table.

2 To eat, place one or two salad leaves in your hand, then a small spoonful of rice, followed by a little sauce and *banchan*. Make a parcel and eat in one bite.

This dish goes particularly well with grilled meats.

Ssam means "wrapped mouthful." However, they are not rolls or dumplings. *Ssam* can only be wrapped in leaves, such as lettuce, romaine, batavia, treviso, mustard leaves or sometimes seaweed.

More difficult to find outside of Korea, fresh perilla leaves or zucchini leaves are often used to make *ssam*.

와구
와구

Hot tip
Going to a ssam restaurant is a bad omen for a romantic first date. In fact, if one of the two people suggests eating ssam, the message here is: "I don't like you that much, no need to make an effort to impress" (actually, talking with your mouth full — full of ssam — goes against the rules of courtesy).

COOKED RiCE DiSHES

Cooked rice dishes have incredible flavor and are a nice change from everyday white rice. They are often made with leftover rice, which is very handy.

김밥 KiMBAP, SEAWEED RiCE ROLL

A sweet, tasty and fun dish, *kimbap* is a snack loved by all and often eaten at picnics. You can add tuna, cooked meats or make them with 100% vegetables.

김밥 말기

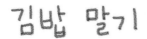

1. Slice 1 cup (150 g) of yellow pickled radishes into long strips (8.5 inches/22 cm) 7 mm thick.

2. Mix 4.23 oz (120 g) of ground beef with a third of the *bulgogi* sauce (see p. 46) and cook in a frying pan. Cook 3 beaten eggs like a flat pancake in a frying pan with a little oil, then cut into strips just under half an inch (1 cm) wide. Cut 1 carrot into 3 mm wide strips and cook in a frying pan with a little oil. Season with salt and pepper.

3. Make 4 servings of rice, following the recipe on p. 31. In a large bowl, fluff the rice by mixing with 1 ½ tbsp (22.5 ml) of rice vinegar, 1 tbsp (15 ml) of toasted sesame oil and 1 tsp (5 ml) of salt.

4. Place 1 sheet of seaweed *gim* on a maki mat. Spread ¼ of the rice on just over half of the seaweed. Put the fillings in the middle one by one. Roll the sheet up, moisten the end of the seaweed with a little water and stick it down.

5. Cut these 4 rolls into slices just over half an inch (1.5 cm) thick and sprinkle with sesame seeds before eating.

BiBiMBAP 비빔밥

It can be very easy to make by topping with the leftover *banchan* and *gochujang* paste, or you can make it a bit fancier and festive for celebrations (see recipe p. 74 - *Bibimbap*).

KiMCHi-BOKKEUMBAP, KiMCHi FRiED RiCE

콩나물국

김치볶음밥

For Koreans, this dish is very common but still delicious. Mix the rice into the sauteed *kimchi* with a little vegetable oil. At this point, you have the option of adding pork, bacon or, in the latest trend, melted cheese. All types of *kimchi* can be used. If you pair this with a soybean sprout soup, you'll have one of the most popular Korean lunches.

BROTHS 육수와 국물

Koreans consider themselves to be big soup-lovers. You will always find a spoon next to the chopsticks. The consistency can either be light like a broth, or thicker like a runny sauce. Dishes with names ending in guk 국 mean that it is a soup in the broad sense of the word. The word tang탕 or jang장 can also be used. In Korean cooking, beef-based broths are most common.

BASICS OF BROTH RECIPES

육수 만들기

집 간장

A bottle of clear soy sauce
Broths are seasoned with salt and/or soy sauce choengjang (p. 55).

Cooking broths is always done with a lid on and starting cold.

For broths made with red meat or bones, soak for 1 hour (4 hours for bones) in a large volume of water to draw out the blood. It is better to pour the water from the first boil away, and put the meat in fresh water to continue cooking. Skim from time to time (1), strain using a fine sieve when you are finished cooking (2), let it cool and, lastly, remove any solidified fats from the surface (3).

Whatever the cooking time, vegetables and herbs should be added 30 minutes before the broth has finished cooking.

The following recipes produce 2.5 to 3 quarts (liters) of broth.

Instant broths (without MSG) are very handy, as they come in packets with dehydrated, natural ingredients.

BASIC BROTHS

Sogogi-yuksu, beef broth

1 Cook 16 oz (450 g) of beef brisket in 4.5 quarts (liters) of water. Once it is boiling, turn the heat down to medium heat, then let it cook for 1 hour.

2 Add just over ½ a cup (90 g) of scallions and 4 cloves of garlic, then continue cooking for another 30 minutes.

3 Remove the meat. It can then be sliced or shredded before being added to a dish.

Myeolchi-yuksu dried anchovies

Toast 1 oz (30 g) of dried anchovies (the type used for broths) for 1 minute, in a dry pan, then remove their intestines. Let 1 oz (30 g) of kombu seaweed and the anchovies infuse in 3.3 quarts (liters) of water for 1 hour. Bring to a boil, turn off the heat, then let it rest for 15 minutes. Strain and season.

Dak-yuksu with chicken

Following the basic steps (see p. 36), prepare 1 chicken or its carcass, 4.5 quarts (liters) of water, just over ½ a cup (90 g) of scallions, 4 cloves of garlic and a small piece of ginger. Let this cook for 1 h 30 m. When using a chicken carcass, a longer cooking time gives a better result.

Sagol-yuksu with beef bones

Following the basic steps (see p. 36), prepare 6.6 lbs (3 kg) of beef bones or marrow, 2.2 lbs (1 kg) of beef tendons, 7 quarts (liters) of water and a pinch of pepper. Let this cook for 6 to 12 hours. Add more water while the soup is still cooking, if needed.

Chaesu with vegetables

Cut just over ¾ cup (100 g) of white radish, and the same amount of scallions with their roots (or onions), ¾ cup (100 g) of carrots, 10 shiitake mushrooms into small pieces, add between ⅓ and ½ a cup (70-100 ml) of soy sauce, 1 chili (optional) and cook for around 15 minutes in 3 quarts (liters) of boiling water. Strain.

Ssalteumul, rice water

Rinse the rice. Pour the water from the first and second rinses away. During the third rinse, agitate the rice by vigorously mixing it with a little water. Save this cloudy water. It will make soups with a fermented soybean paste (p. 18 and 19) or stewed vegetable base milder.

Donchimi-gukmul, kimchi water as a broth

This broth is used in cold noodle soups, especially *naengmyeon* (p. 61).

37

LiGHT SOUPS

구
국

In everyday meals, guk, the soup, is paired with rice; they are always served together. In general, soups are generously garnished with vegetables and seasoned with salty fermented sauces (soy sauce, doenjang or fermented fish sauce).

미역국

Miyeok-guk

시금치국

Sigeumchi-doenjang-guk

콩나물국

Kongnamul-guk

오이냉국

Oii-nenguk

Miyeok-guk, seaweed soup

1 Rehydrate 0.7 oz (20 g) of seaweed *miyeok* (wakamé) in 1 quart (liter) of water for 10 minutes and then cut it into 1.5 inch (4 cm) pieces. Cut 3 oz (80 g) of beef shin into small pieces, mix the meat with ½ tsp (2.5 ml) of minced garlic, 1 tsp (5 ml) of *cheongjang* sauce and 1 tbsp (15 ml) of toasted sesame oil. Let it marinate for 10 minutes.

2 Cook the meat for 2 minutes on medium heat in a large saucepan without any fat. Stir in the seaweed and continue cooking for 3 minutes. Add 1.5 quarts (liters) of water, 2 tsp (10 ml) of *cheongjang* sauce and let it cook with the lid on for 20 minutes. Add 2 tbsp (30 ml) of chopped scallions, a pinch of pepper and adjust the seasoning if needed.

Sigeumchi-doenjang-guk, fermented soybean paste soup with spinach

Dilute just under ¼ cup (60 g) of *doenjang* in 2 ½ cups (650 ml) of beef or anchovy broth, add 2 ½ cups (650 ml) of rice water (see p. 37). Bring this to a boil over medium heat. Add 8.5 oz (250 g) of medium-firm tofu cut into ¾ inch (2 cm) cubes and 1 tsp (5 ml) of minced garlic, then 3 handfuls of baby spinach 2 minutes later. Continue cooking for 2 minutes, add 2 tbsp (30 ml) of chopped scallions to finish.

Kongnamul-guk with soybean sprouts

This is one of the most popular soups amongst Koreans, due to its refreshing taste and affordable price. You can make it with anchovy or beef broth (see p. 37).

Simplified recipe: cook 1 cup (150 g) of soybean sprouts in 1.3 quarts (liters) of anchovy broth, flavor with a little garlic and chopped scallions when finished cooking. Season with salt.

Oii-nenguk, cold cucumber soup

Put 2 tbsp (30 ml) of *cheongjang* sauce, 1 tbsp (15 ml) of rice vinegar, 3 tbsp (45 ml) chopped scallions, 1 tsp (5 ml) of sugar, 1 tsp (5 ml) of chopped red chili, 2 ½ cups (300 g) of grated cucumber and 1 tsp (5 ml) of toasted sesame seeds in just under 3 ½ cups (800 ml) of cold water. Mix together and adjust the seasoning with salt. Serve right away.

JEONGOL, HOT POT 전골

Delicious and fun, this dish is also very easy to make, as all you have to do is put raw ingredients and some broth in a large saucepan. Guests cook their own food at the table.

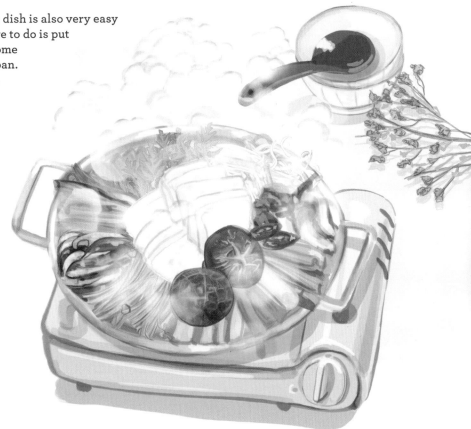

Beoseot-jeongol, mushroom and tofu hot pot 버섯전골

1 Prepare 3 ¾ cups (600 g) of mixed mushrooms: *eryngii*, girolles, shiitakes, *enoki*, Paris mushrooms, etc. Cut 17.5 oz (500 g) of medium-firm tofu into 1.5 inch (4 cm) squares, with a width of less than ½ an inch (1 cm).

2 Cut ¾ cup (100 g) of carrots, ¾ cup (100 g) scallions, ¾ cup (100 g) of zucchini and ¾ cup (100 g) of *minari* (see p. 16) into strips around 2 inches (5-6 cm) long, not too thick.

3 Neatly place half of each ingredient in a large, rather deep saucepan and pour in just over 2 cups (500 ml) of beef or vegetable broth (see p. 37).

4 Set up the camping stove in the middle of the table, put the prepared saucepan on top and cook over medium heat.

5 Place small ladles, individual bowls, soy sauce and pepper in front of each of your guests. As soon as the vegetables are cooked, everyone serves themselves at their own convenience.

6 As the saucepan gradually empties, refill it with the remaining ingredients and just over 2 cups (500 ml) of broth.

7 This dish is eaten with rice and *kimchi*.

HEARTY SOUPS 찌개

Jjigae 찌개 is a dish somewhere in between a stew and soup. The broth used is thicker than that used for guk. The flavor is also more concentrated and works perfectly as a sauce for rice.

CHEONGGUKJANG-JJIGAE, INSTANT FERMENTED SOYBEAN SOUP

Dish with cheonggukjang and doenjang.

청국장 찌개

Recipe

1. In a saucepan, dilute 2 tbsp (30 g) of *doenjang* and 1 ½ tbsp (22.5 g) of *cheonggukjang* (see *jang* p. 57) with 1 ½ cups (350 ml) of anchovy broth and 1 ½ cups (350 ml) of rice water (see p. 37).

2. Add ¾ cup (100 g) of *kimchi* cut into small pieces, its water and ¾ cup (100 g) of sliced shiitake mushrooms. Bring this to a boil over medium heat. Once it's boiling, add 7 oz (200 g) of medium-firm tofu cut into ¾ inch (2 cm) cubes and 1 tsp (5 ml) of minced garlic. Continue cooking for a few minutes, then turn off the heat. Add another 2 tbsp (30 g) of *cheonggukjang* and 2 tbsp (30 ml) of chopped scallions. Serve hot with rice.

김치찌개

Kimchi-jjigae, kimchi soup

In a saucepan, sauté 4.2 oz (120 g) of pork shoulder cut into small pieces in sesame oil for 3 minutes, stir in 1 ½ cups (250 g) of sliced *kimchi* (with its liquid) and 1 tsp (5 ml) of *gochugaru* (optional), and continue cooking for 1 minute. Add just under 3 ½ cups (800 ml) of water, 10.5 oz (300 g) of tofu cut into ¾ inch (2 cm) cubes and 1 small sliced onion. Cook for 5 minutes over high heat. Add just under ¼ cup (20 g) of chopped scallions when finished cooking.

Sundubu-jjigae, tofu soup with seafood

This soup is always served in an individual clay pot. Enjoy the contrast between the spiced broth and the mild silken tofu.

순두부찌개

In a clay pot, sauté 1 tsp (5 ml) minced garlic, 2 to 4 tsp (10-20 ml) of *gochugaru*, ⅓ of a tsp (1.5 ml) of chopped ginger in a mix of 2 tsp (10 ml) of toasted sesame oil and 2 tsp (10 ml) of plain vegetable oil for 30 seconds. Let these ingredients sauté for 30 seconds, while adding 1 tbsp (15 ml) of *cheongjang* sauce and 3 handfuls of clams. Then add 2 ½ cups (600 ml) of anchovy broth (see p. 37), 10.5 oz (300 g) of silken tofu and 1 tsp (5 ml) of *saeujeot* (see p. 18). Season with salt if needed. Once it is boiling, crack 1 egg and turn off the heat. Add 2 tbsp (30 ml) of chopped scallions and some sliced fresh chili (optional).

BUDAE-JJIGAE, ARMY STEW

1 In a saucepan, place 1 handful of *kimchi* in small pieces, 7 oz (200 g) of sliced Montbéliard sausage (or SPAM®), 4 sliced Frankfurt sausages, 8 slices of bacon cut into small pieces, 1 chopped onion and 1 handful of rice cakes (*toppoki* - see p. 71).

부대찌개

2 Mix in 2 tbsp (30 ml) of *gochujang*, 2 tbsp (30 ml) of soy sauce, 1 tbsp (15 ml) of *gochugaru*, 2 tsp (10 ml) of minced garlic, 2 tsp (10 ml) of sugar. Place all of these ingredient in a saucepan with 3 cups (700 ml) of water and cook over medium heat.

3 Once it's boiling, add 3.5 oz (100 g) of *ramyeon* noodles (p. 68), 1 ½ cups (100 g) of cooked navy beans, 2 tbsp (30 ml) of chopped scallions. Adjust the amount of water. Turn off the heat when the noodles are cooked.

나물 반찬
NAMUL BANCHAN: VEGETABLES

Namul refers to all sorts of simple vegetable dishes. It's an essential part of banchan. With one simple vegetable, you can make a variety of delicious dishes. There are four main cooking techniques.

BLANCH-SEASONING METHOD

데친 나물

For green vegetables and sprouts.

Basic recipe

1. In a large saucepan of salted, boiling water, blanch 2 to 3 cups (300-400 g) of vegetables: 2 minutes for spinach, 5 minutes for soybean sprouts, then rinse and squeeze to get rid of any excess water. The cooking time varies depending on the vegetable, bearing in mind that it's best to keep a slight crunch.

2. Season with salt, 1 tsp (5 ml) of crushed garlic, 2 tsp (10 ml) of chopped scallions, 2 or 3 tsp (10-15 ml) of toasted sesame oil (or toasted perilla oil) and some sesame seeds.

3. You can mix it up by adding some chili powder, or by replacing the salt with *cheongjang* sauce.

Sesame spinach

Soybean sprouts

Mung bean sprouts

BRAISING IN SOY SAUCE 조림

Basic recipe

1. Chop 3 cups (450 g) of potatoes into chestnut-sized pieces.

2. In a bowl, mix just over 1 cup (250 ml) of water, ½ a tsp (2.5 ml) of crushed garlic, 3 tbsp (45 ml) of soy sauce, 1 tbsp (15 ml) of honey, 1 tbsp (15 ml) of sugar and 1 tbsp (15 ml) of sesame oil.

3. Briefly sauté the potatoes in 1 tbsp (15 ml) of oil. Pour in the sauce and cook them for about ten minutes, keeping them covered. Sprinkle toasted sesame seeds on top.

4. Cooking lotus roots: peel 1 ½ cups (300 g) of lotus roots and cut them into slices 3 mm thick, then let them soak for 20 minutes in 1 quart (liter) of water with 3 tbsp (45 ml) of vinegar. Pat them dry then cook them in the same way as the potatoes.

Yeongeun-jorim, lotus root braised soy sauce.

Gamja-jorim, potatoes braised in soy sauce.

FRY-SEASONING METHOD

볶음

Gosari-namul,
fern sprouts
pan-fried in perilla oil

Aehobak-namul,
pan-fried Korean zucchini

Beoseot-namul,
pan-fried mushrooms

1 Cut 2 to 3 cups (300-400 g) of vegetables into slices or small, short strips, not too thick.

2 Sauté them for 1 to 2 minutes with 1 tsp (5 ml) of crushed garlic in a frying pan with a little vegetable oil on low heat. Cook the ingredients down until they are tender. Season with salt. Turn off the heat, add 2 tbsp (30 ml) of chopped scallions and ground toasted sesame seeds.

Cooking fern sprouts: the day before, boil 1.5 quarts (liters) of water. Turn the heat off, add ¾ cup (50 g) of dried fern sprouts and let them soak overnight, covered. The next day, drain them, remove the tough parts and rinse, then use them like you would any other fresh vegetable. To season, substitute salt with *cheongjang* sauce.

RAW SALAD METHOD

생채

Pa-muchim, tender scallion salad, hot sauce: soak thin strips of scallion in water for 10 minutes, pat them dry and dress with a sweet soy sauce vinaigrette, then add chili flakes for a little spice.

Doragi-nengchae, platycodon root salad: cut the root into matchsticks, rub with salt and soak for 1 hour in water to get rid of any bitterness. Enjoy with a pine nut and mustard dressing (see p. 19).

Geotjeori, lettuce with a *spicy* kimchi dressing: ready-made *kimchi* or salad with a *kimchi*-style sauce. This dish is eaten right away, without any fermentation.

BANCHAN: SEAWEEDS, TOFU AND JELLIES

해초 두부 묵

Seaweed is an important part of Korean cuisine due to its iodine flavor and smooth texture. There are fifty or so edible varieties in Korea and plenty of regional recipes to enjoy.

GIM-GUI, SEAWEED CHIPS 김구이

Found in almost all everyday meals, they are used to wrap small bites of rice.

Basic recipe

1. On a tray, thinly cover a sheet of seaweed with oil (sesame or perilla) and sprinkle with salt. Prepare several sheets in the same way.

2. Toast them one by one for several seconds on each side in a dry frying pan by pressing on them with a spatula until the color becomes a more transparent green. Take them off the heat before there are any signs of burning.

3. Cut them into eight sections with a pair of scissors.

❶

❷

❸

다시마쌈

Dashima ssam
Dashima seaweed rice (p. 17) rolls, with cho-gochujang sauce (see p. 19)

미역무침
Miyeok-muchim
Miyeok seaweed salad (p. 17) enhanced with a sweet and sour dressing and sesame oil.

Tofu goes well with all sauces and is an excellent source of protein in the often vegetarian Korean diet.

두부 만들기

Making tofu - step by step

1 To make 10.5 oz (300 g) of tofu, you will need about ¾ cup (100 g) of dried soybeans. Soak them for 8 hours, then grind them down. Strain and save the milk.

2 Heat it up.

3 Coagulate by adding magnesium chloride.

4 Drain and press to make a block.

Mongeul-mongeul sundubu, soft, fresh tofu curds
Soup with tofu curds, before straining. This is diluted with yangnyeom-ganjang sauce (see p. 19).

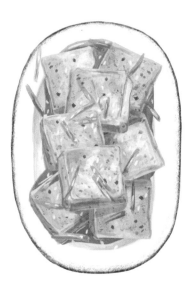

Dubu-jorim 두부조림, tofu braised in spicy sauce

1 On a plate, lay out 10.5 oz (300 g) of 1.5 inch (4 cm) tofu squares, less than half an inch (1 cm) wide, season with salt and leave for 10 minutes to draw out any excess water. Pat dry. In just under ½ a cup (100 ml) of water, mix 1 tsp (5 ml) of minced garlic, 1 tsp (5 ml) of perilla oil, 2 tsp (10 ml) of sugar, ½ tsp (2.5 ml) of *gochugaru* and 5 tsp (25 ml) of soy sauce. Season with pepper.

2 In a pre-heated frying pan over medium heat, brown the tofu with a little perilla oil and pour in the sauce. Let it cook and baste with the sauce from time to time.

3 When the sauce has reduced by half, turn off the heat. Stir in 2 tbsp (30 ml) of chopped scallions and a few toasted sesame seeds.

Dotorimuk-muchim, acorn jelly salad
Enjoy the woody smell of the oak and its astringent and tannin-like flavor. It is eaten with yangnyeom-ganjang sauce.

도토리묵

고기반찬

BANCHAN: MEATS

Although, nowadays, more meat is used in everyday banchan, it is generally a "secondary" or less important component: it is eaten in small servings, chopped or ground, mixed with vegetables or used to garnish soups. Here are some dishes where the main ingredient is meat.

HOMEMADE BULGOGI, KOREAN MARINATED BEEF

1 In a large bowl, mix 2 tbsp (30 ml) of chopped scallions, 2 tsp (10 ml) of crushed garlic, 2 tsp (10 ml) of ground toasted sesame seeds, 2 tbsp (30 ml) of sugar, just under ¼ cup (50 ml) of pear juice, 3 tbsp (45 ml) of soy sauce and 1 tbsp (15 ml) of toasted sesame oil.

2 Add 14 oz (400 g) of thinly sliced sirloin steak and 1 sliced onion, mix and let marinate for 20 minutes.

3 In a hot frying pan, cook the meat for 3 to 6 minutes. Serve right away with a green salad and *ssam-jang* sauce (see p. 19), ssam-style (see p. 33).

Marinade ingredients

소불고

장조림

Jang-jorim, preserved beef in soy sauce
Preserved beef brisket, cut into thin "shredded" strips. This dish is served in very small quantities as the taste is so concentrated.

JEYUK-BOKKEUM, MARINATED PORK 제육볶음

This is a variation of *bulgogi*, made with pork and *gochujang* (chili paste) sauce.

1. In a large bowl, mix 1 to 2 tbsp (15 to 30 ml) of *gochujang*, 2 tsp (10 ml) of *gochujaru*, ½ a tsp (2.5 ml) of chopped ginger, 1 tbsp (15 ml) of chopped scallions, 1 tsp (5 ml) of crushed garlic, 2 tsp (10 ml) of sugar, 2 tbsp (30 ml) of soy sauce, 2 tbsp (30 ml) of rice wine and 2 tbsp (30 ml) of toasted sesame oil.

2. Add just over 1 lb. (500 g) of thinly sliced pork shoulder and 1 sliced green chili, mix and let marinate for 20 minutes.

3. Cook the meat in a hot frying pan. If it's too dry, add some water. Sprinkle toasted sesame seeds on top. Serve right away with a green salad, *ssam*-style (see p. 33).

닭찜

Dak-jjim, braised chicken with soy sauce
This uses the same kind of seasoning as *bulgogi*, but with chicken. The vegetables are cut into large pieces and stewed.

해산물

BANCHAN: FISH AND SEAFOOD

Korea is the largest consumer of fish in the world. Thanks to its geographical location, it has access to a wide variety of seafood products. It is prepared fresh, dried or salt-cured and eaten raw, cooked or fermented. Koreans are very demanding when it comes to freshness and fish is rarely sold in fillets. For banchan, it is grilled, preserved in soy sauce or used to garnish soups.

The five most commonly eaten fish are mackerel, squid, sabre tooth fish, shrimp and flounder. However, the most popular in home cooking is the anchovy. It is affordable, versatile (preserved, in broths, as a snack to nibble on, paired with an alcoholic drink...) and easy to store.

멸치볶음

Myeolchi-bokkeum, small dried anchovies preserved in soy sauce.

멸치 종류

There are three types of anchovies depending on how you're using them: the smallest is for preserving, the largest is for broths and the medium-sized is versatile.

48

GODEUNGEO-JORIM, MACKEREL AND PRESERVED RADISH

고등어조림

1 In a large saucepan, spread 2 ½ cups (400 g) of white radish, cut into 1-inch (3 cm) squares 7 mm thick, then place 2 large mackerel fillets on top.

2 In a bowl, mix 6 tbsp (90 ml) of soy sauce, 2 tsp (10 ml) of crushed garlic, 1 tsp (5 ml) of chopped ginger, 2 tbsp (30 ml) of sugar, 1 tbsp (15 ml) of *gochugaru* and 1 tbsp (15 ml) of *soju* (see p. 125). Pour just under 1 cup (200 ml) of water over the fish, then the sauce. Cook for 15 minutes on medium heat, keeping it covered. Add 3 tbsp (45 ml) of chopped scallions, continue to cook until the radish is tender and the sauce has thickened.

Ojingeo-bokkeum, stir fried squid with vegetables in gochujang sauce.

오징어볶음

갈치구이

Galchi-gui, grilled sabre tooth fish.

Comak-muchim, steamed cockles and seasoned soy sauce (see p. 19 - Sauces).

꼬막무침

달걀 BANCHAN: EGGS

In a meal without fish, a dish with eggs provides a great source of animal protein. Recently, with the explosion of spicy dishes, egg has become a popular addition due to its sweet flavor.

알찜

Aljjim, silky egg flan

A true classic in traditional cooking. The egg is strained and gently steamed, then seasoned with fermented shrimp liquid.

뚝배기 계란찜

Ttukbaegi-gyeranjjim, steamed in a clay pot

Thanks to the clay pot and its lid, you get a light texture with only eggs and water.

Japchae

Ramyeon, instant noodles: to make up for its lack of nutritious value and enhance this mass-produced product.

Kimchi-bokkeumbap, kimchi fried rice: the mild flavor of the egg counteracts the acidity of the kimchi.

In traditional *obangsaek* tradition (see p. 10), the egg acts as a finishing touch with its yellow color (egg strips, whole raw yolk...).

달걀조림

Preserved egg in soy sauce

DALGYAL-MARI, EGG ROLL

달걀말이

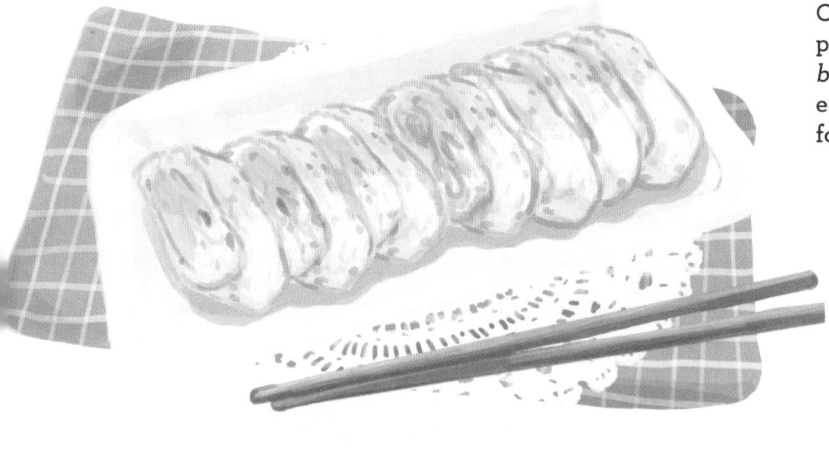

One of the most common, popular and nutritious *banchan* options. To be eaten with rice and *kimchi* for a complete dish.

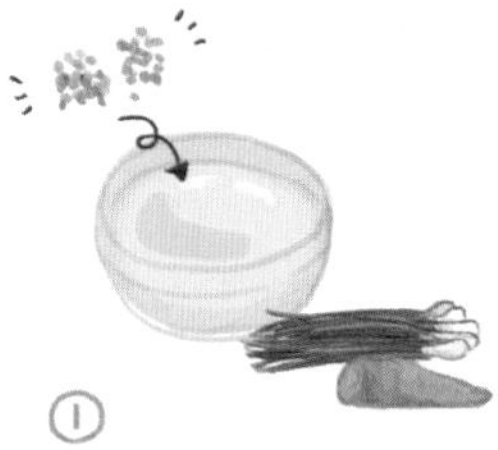

①

1 Pass 8 eggs through a sieve. Season with salt, pepper and add ¼ cup (4 tbsp) of carrots and ¼ cup (4 tbsp) of scallions, both finely chopped.

2 Heat a frying pan over high heat. When it is really hot, turn the heat down to the lowest setting. Coat the pan with oil.

3 Spread a quarter of the egg and fold it over to a width of 1.5 inches (4 cm) using a spatula. Slide the egg roll to the side of the pan and coat the pan with oil again.

4 Pour the second quarter of the egg - pour it so that the end of the first egg roll overlaps with the second.

5 Continue to roll, each time leaving a small part sticking out. Slide the roll to the side of the pan. Pour the third quarter of the egg in, then continue to roll by repeating the same process.

6 Fry each side of the roll for 2 minutes. Remove from the pan and let the roll cool for a moment, then cut it into ½ an inch (1 to 2 cm) slices.

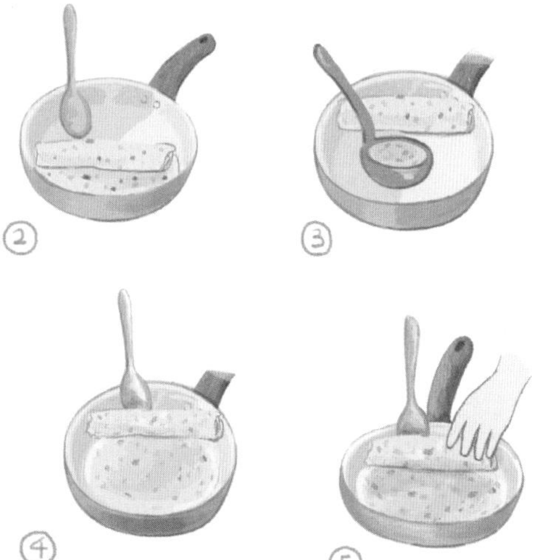

② ③ ④ ⑤

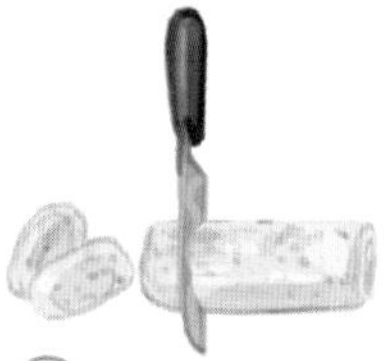

⑥

발효 음식

FERMENTATION

In Korea, fermentation experts do not hesitate to call themselves "nature alchemists." They are, according to them, capable of detecting from the surrounding environment the perfect conditions for the fermentation of their jang: the famous fermented condiment, the foundation of Korean cooking.

They also use fermented clay to make pots and vases in which the kimchi and jang are left to mature over the seasons, the time required for maturation.

장 JANG: FERMENTED CONDIMENTS

Without fermented foods, Korean cuisine would lose its charm; they shaped the Korean palate while providing essential nutrients.

It's also a spiritual tradition. Before scientific discoveries linked to the fermentation process (the presence of bacteria, etc.), people believed mysterious forces (their ancestors, considered to be guardian angels) kindly intervened in the process. Fermentation has, without doubt, promoted a sensitivity to the invisible and mysterious world, stemming from spiritual experiences, without scientific explanation.

Jangdokdae, a fermented food store and home to the household protective spirit Ancestors went there to get their jang, but also to make wishes. An upside down sock would trap bad spells. In fact, their white color reflected the light into dark corners helping to cleanse the space.

장독대

Doenjang, fermented soybean paste

Jang, 장, refers to condiments fermented with salt, usually made with soy sauce. In Korean cooking, they are as important as salt. They are eaten in soups, and sauces. They sometimes act as a replacement for salt and can be used as a household remedy.

Their umami flavor, derived from soy protein and digested by microorganisms, adds flavor to vegetarian meals and rice.

콩

Yellow, black and green soybeans

Three types of soybean
This legume is native to Manchuria, where the ancient Korean kingdoms were once found. In these vegetarian, Buddhist countries, soybeans were used as an essential source of protein. Very early on, they were consumed fermented, as non-fermented soybeans are hard to digest.

TYPES OF FERMENTED SOY CONDIMENTS

된장

Doenjang:
fermented soybean paste

고추장

Gochujang: fermented soybean paste with chili

청국장

Cheonggukjang: instant fermented soybeans

간장 Ganjangs : soy sauce - 3 types:

Clear, maturation less than a year (cheongjang)

Medium, maturation is between 1 to 4 years (jungjang)

Matured (jinjang)

MAKING TRADITIONAL DOENJANG AND GANJANG

장 담그기

The natural fermentation process, without using a starter culture, requires a lot of experience to know how to adapt to the natural environmental conditions. Therefore, it is not surprising that each batch tastes different, proof of the microbial diversity that is beneficial for our health. This natural method is unpredictable and expensive. Nowadays, factories produce *jangs* by using simplified microbes. This means that the taste is more consistent and the fermentation time is shorter, between 3 to 12 months.

1 Cooking.

2 Grinding.

3 Shaping.

4 First fermentation in a cool place in direct con with rice straw: 1 mo

5 Second warm fermentation: 1 month.

메주

6 Meju: ready-made soybean starter.

7 Third fermentation in brine: 2 or 3 months.

8 Straining, the solids are the doenjang and the liquid is ganjang.

Sauce soja

Doenjan

9 Maturation: 1 to 5 years or more.

GOCHUJANG, FERMENTED SOYBEAN PASTE WITH CHILI

Although chilis were not introduced to Korea until around the 17th century, their sweet and spicy flavor quickly charmed the Koreans. The famous fried chicken and *toppoki* would not exist today if *gochujang* had not been created.

Fresh chilis in gochujang. Did you know? Koreans eat fresh chilis in chili sauce!

Gochujang ingredients: powdered meju, rice flour, malt, rice syrup, chili powder and salt.

CHEONGGUKJANG, INSTANT FERMENTED SOY 청국장

This type of soy is the result of a short fermentation (1 to 4 years) without salt. People's opinions on this product are divided. Some are fervent fans and others are grouchy critics who dislike its strong smell, but it is unanimously praised for its dietary benefits. It is eaten cooked, in stews (see recipe p. 40), but also as tablets to supplement your diet.

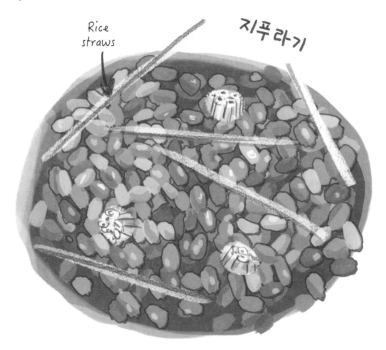

Rice straws

지푸라기

청국장 띄우기

37 ~ 40 °C

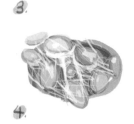

1. In a saucepan, let 1 ½ cups (200 g) of rinsed, organic yellow soybeans soak for 8 hours in 2 ½ cups (600 ml) of water.

2. Bring this to the boil and continue to cook over low heat, with the lid on, until the pulses are tender (3-4 hours). Stir regularly. Add more water if needed. When it is finished, all the water should be absorbed, but the soybeans should still be very moist. Turn the heat off.

3. Mix with 2 or 3 rice straws or 1 tsp (5 ml) of raw brown rice. Spread the soybeans out in a large container, between ½ - 1 inch (2 cm) thick. Put a piece of paper underneath the lid to absorb condensation (it should not touch the soybeans). Close the lid.

4. Let this heat up to 95 - 102 °F (35 - 39 °C) for 1 to 4 hours.

5. A white layer and a cheese-like smell appear. Strings are formed when the beans are stirred.

6. To eat raw, 1 or 2 days of fermentation is enough.

EVERYTHING ABOUT KIMCHI 김치

The predecessors of kimchi were probably vegetables simply fermented with salt, a universal preservation method. The unique Korean trend started with the use of fermented soybeans instead of salt.

The invention of the complex spice blend, specific to *kimchi*, goes back about 500 years. Both internationally and in Korea, *baechu kimchi*, pe-tsaï cabbage with *gochugaru* (chili flakes), is the most well-known and most commonly consumed. Its current form dates back about 200 years. In the past, the cabbage variety was different, pepper or mustard were used as seasoning, and chili wasn't so readily available.

Traditional kimchi container.

김장

Kimjang, winter kimchi

In winter, fermented vegetables provide vitamins and nutrients. Preserved in underground jars (containers perfect for *kimchi*, from 32 - 33.8 °F (0 to 1 °C) even in winter, as in Korea the temperature can easily drop to below 14 or even 4 °F (-10 to -20 °C) in the North), you can get delicious vegetables that are as good as fresh produce.

Making *kimjang* is an annual community ritual, consolidating social bonds, and it is registered on the UNESCO world heritage list.

MAKING KIMCHI WITH A WHOLE CABBAGE

 1)    2)    3)   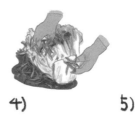 4)    5)

1. Dissolve just under ½ a cup (100 g) of sea salt in 1 quart (liter) of water, cut 2 lbs (1 kg) of Napa cabbage into halves or quarters and place in the water. Let marinate for 6 hours, stirring regularly. Pull the thicker leaves close to the core apart so that the brine can be absorbed.

2. Rinse thoroughly with fresh water and let dry for 10 minutes.

3. In a bowl, put around 2 tbsp (20 to 30 g) of *gochugaru*, 2 to 3 tsp (10-15 ml) of minced garlic, 1 tsp (5 ml) of chopped ginger, 1 tbsp (15 ml) of sugar, 1 tbsp (15 ml) of fermented fish sauce (or soy sauce), 1 cup (150 g) of white radish cut into matchsticks, 2 tsp (10 ml) of rice flour boiled in ⅓ cup (70 ml) of water (optional) and ¼ cup (40 g) of chopped scallions. Mix all the ingredients together.

4. Set a large cabbage leaf to the side. Spread the sauce between all the cabbage leaves.

5. Place the cabbage in a container, tightly packed, without any air pockets. Leave just over an inch (3 cm) between the cabbage leaves and the lid.

6. Cover the contents with the large cabbage leaf you set aside earlier (keep it until you have finished).

7. Close the container, let it ferment for 2 days at room temperature, then put it in the refrigerator. You can start eating it on the 5th day. After 2 or 3 weeks, the taste should be perfect.

Bear in mind: for making fermented foods, Uniodized, non-fluoridated sea salt is recommended.

For *white* kimchi: replace *gochugaru* with some strands (or slices) of dried chili.

백김치

Baek kimchi, pe-tsaï cabbage white kimchi

Baechu pogi kimchi, pe-tsaï cabbage kimchi with a whole chili

Makkimchi, 막김치 easy baechu kimchi

Cut the cabbage into 1-1.5 inch (3 or 4 cm) pieces. Then, continue in the same way as for the whole cabbage recipe, but the brining time will be shorter, around 3 hours. After drying, mix the cabbage with the sauce.

KKAKTUGI, PEAR OR WHITE RADISH KIMCHI

깍두기

The white radish version goes well with *seolleongtang* (see p. 76).

1 In a large bowl, mix 6 ¼ cups (500 g) of Asian pears cut into half an inch (1.5 cm) cubes with 2 tsp (10 g) of sea salt and leave for 30 minutes to draw out any excess water, then pat them dry.

2 In a large bowl, mix 2 tsp (10 g) of *gochugaru*, ½ a tsp (2.5 ml) of chopped ginger, ½ a tsp (2.5 ml) of minced garlic 1 tbsp (15 ml) of soy sauce. Add to the pear along with 1.5 cups (20 g) of chopped scallions. Mix together.

3 Place, tightly packed, in a 17 oz (500 ml) jar. Leave a little space between the pear and the lid. Close and ensure it is airtight.

4 Let ferment for 2 days at room temperature, then refrigerate for at least 1 week. *Kkaktugi* will keep fresh for 1 month or more.

or

　①　　②　　③　

NABAK-KIMCHI, KIMCHI WITH SPICED WATER

나박김치

1 Cut 2 ½ cups (300 g) of Napa cabbage into 1-1.5 inch (3 to 4 cm) pieces. Marinate them for 2 hours in just over 2 cups (500 ml) of salty water, using 3.5 tbsp (50 g) of sea sa Rinse thoroughly and let dry for 5 minutes.

2 In a large bowl, dissolve 2 tsp (10 g) of salt in 2 ½ cups (600 m of water, add 1 tsp (5 ml) of *gochugaru*, 1 tbsp (15 ml) of white sugar, 1 tsp (5 ml) of crushed garlic, ½ a tsp (2.5 ml) of choppe ginger, 1 tbsp (15 g) of scallions and ¼ cup (30 g) of *minari* (see p. 16) cut into 1 inch (3 cm) pieces and ½ cup (70 g) of white radish cut into 1 inch (3 cm) by 3 mm cubes, as well as th brined cabbage. Pour it all into a 1 quart (liter) jar, and close it

3 Let it ferment for 2 days at room temperature, then keep in the fridge for 1 to 3 weeks.

　①　　②　　③

HOW TO STORE KIMCHI AND HOW TO USE IT

Electric kimchi refrigerator

When you place the *kimchi* in the container, press down to remove any air pockets. The liquid must cover the *kimchi* in order to prevent any contact with air, which would soften the texture of the vegetable. If there is not enough liquid, pour in a little 2% brine, ½ tsp salt/just under ½ cup of water (2 g of salt/100 ml of water). Cover the contents with a large cabbage leaf.

The fermentation time varies depending on the temperature of the room. ou can try it on the fifth day, when the fermented flavor - acidity - appears. If you want to achieve a ore intense flavor, wait a little longer. As a guide, for a 1 quart (liter) jar of *kimchi*, a period of 2 or 3 eeks is ideal; it will be pleasantly acidic, crunchy and rich in nutrients.

he shelf life can vary from months to years as long as there is acidity; however, the *kimchi* will lose s flavor and nutritional value.
hen the *kimchi* is too old and too acidic, cook it with sweet ingredients: rice, meat, eggs or egetables.

Uses for old kimchi

Kimchi-jeon, flat kimchi pancakes
Tangy pancake with crunchy kimchi, topped with pork or cheese.

Kimchi dumplings
Follow the recipe for meat dumplings (see p. 71) and replace the mung bean sprouts with chopped kimchi.

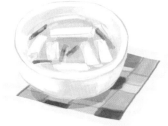

동치미

Dongchimi, kimchi with radishes for broths

The water is used for broths in a variety of noodle dishes or as a hangover cure.

1. In a bowl, mix 2 lbs (1 kg) of white radish cut into 2 inch (5 cm) batons, less than ½ an inch (1 cm) wide, with 2.5 tbsp (40 g) of sea salt. Leave for 15 minutes to draw out any excess water and drain in a sieve.

2. In a large, 96 oz (3 liter) jar, add 2.5 tbsp (40 g) of sea salt, 2.5 tbsp (40 g) scallions cut into 2 inch (5 cm) pieces, 4 cloves of minced garlic, 2 tsp (10 ml) of chopped ginger, ½ a pear and ½ an apple cut into large pieces, 1 chopped onion, 4 fermented (or pickled) green chilis, 1 chopped red chili, then the brined radish. Fill it with water, leaving a 1.5 inch (4 cm) gap at the top, dissolve the salt and close the lid. Let it ferment for 2 days at room temperature, it can then be stored in the refrigerator for at least 1 month.

KIMCHI BY REGION

한국의 김치

Yeolmu-kimchi,
with young white
radish sprouts

Hobak-kimchi,
with pumpkin

Hwang

Sé

Gye

Kkaktugi,
with white radish

Oï-sobagi,
with cucumber

Chungcheong

Nabak-kimchi,
with spiced water

Gaji-kimchi,
with eggplant

Jeolla

Gyeongsang

Jeju

Gyul-kimchi,
with clementines

B.

Baechu kimchi
(both),
with seasoned
pe-tsaï cabbage

Ketnip kimch
with perilla
leaves

Bossam kimchi,
pe-tsaï cabbage
kimchi surprise

Baek kimchi,
with pe-tsaï cabbage

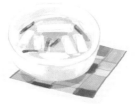

Dongchimi, white
radish water kimchi

Pyongan

Hamgyong

Kangwon

Jangwon

Sikhae, radish, dried
fish and millet kimchi

Andong-sikhye,
kimchi-style drink
with white radish,
rice, malt and chili
water

Kongnip kimchi,
with soybean leaves

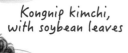

Pa kimchi, with
scallions

OTHER FERMENTED PRODUCTS

Seafood, fruit and grains also have their own types of fermentation. Matured for several years, they become effective flavor enhancers, for example, gaejang (see p. 88), is known as a "rice thief" because it's so tasty your food will be gone in no time.

식해
Sikhae
Fish with fermented vegetables and grains: a type of kimchi

젓갈
Jeotgal
Seafood fermented in salt, fermented shrimp, fish sauce, anchovies.

명란젓

Myeonlan-jeot
Fermented fish roe.

삭힌 홍어
Sakin-hongoe
Fermented skate, it is the Korean equivalent of French maroilles cheese in terms of smell!

Apart from *kimchi* and soybeans, other vegetables are fermented using different methods: drinks, vinegars, and even alcohols.

안동식혜

Andong-sikhye
A kimchi-style drink, with rice and malted barley, flavored with white radish.

식초

Vinegars
Based on makkoli, rice beer (see p. 124) and persimmon.

Cheong **청**
Fermented vegetable syrup (see p. 121) with honey or sugar.

JANGAJJI WITH GARLIC 장아찌

Soy sauce is used to preserve vegetables like garlic or soybean leaf *jangajji*.

1. In a 17 oz (500 ml) Le Parfait®-style jar, pour just under ½ a cup (100 ml) of soy sauce to dissolve 2 tbsp (30 ml) of sugar.

2. Separate 2 to 3 cups (300-400 g) of garlic cloves (small in size), place them in a jar and add some peppercorns. Fill with water and leave a ¾ inch (2 cm) gap below the lid. Let stand for 3 days at room temperature.

3. Keep only the water, pour into a saucepan and bring to a boil with a lid on. Put the cool liquid in a jar. Let marinate for 3 months in a cool place before consuming.

국수와 만두

DOUGH AND NOODLES

Wheat is not a Korean resource, therefore, it is rarely used in traditional recipes. While rice was eaten frequently, noodles and doughs were rare delicacies, saved for special occasions.

Nowadays, wheat imports and local rice production are huge and flour-based foods have become both more readily-available and popular. They now come under the bunsik category, "fast-food," but are also known as "flour meals."

GUKSU, NOODLES

For Koreans, a typical meal usually includes rice. Noodle dishes are mostly eaten as "snacks."

TYPES OF NOODLE

Buckwheat noodles: can be eaten cold or hot.

메밀면

Naengmyeon buckwheat noodles.

냉면국수 (메밀)

Dangmyeon sweet potato starch noodles, for japchae (see p. 69).

당면

Naengmyeon noodles made from starch.

냉면국수 (녹말)

Wheat noodles, thin wheat noodles for janchi-guksu and bibim-guksu (see p. 69).

소면

Wheat noodles for jjajang-myeon (see p. 110)

밀면

Naengmyeon, cold buckwheat noodles (see p. 108), are extremely popular among the older generation, while instant ramyeon (see p. 111) is a creative, fusion dish loved by young people. Noodles spark real passion in Koreans.

Springy wheat noodles.

쫄면

Fried, instant wheat noodles for ramyeon.

라면

Tips for making noodles

1. Put the noodles in boiling, salty water and stir.

2. As soon as the bubbles start to rise vigorously, pour in a glass of cold water and stir. Repeat the same process 3 times, each time the water starts to rise.

3. Pour the cooked noodles into a sieve and rinse several times with cool water.

4. Use them just as they are. For hot dishes, add them to a hot broth.

JAPCHAE VERMICELLI NOODLES WITH VEGETABLES

잡채

Vegetarian recipe

1. Soak 3.5 oz (100 g) of *dangmyeon* noodles in 1 quart (liter) of hot water for 30 minutes.

2. Prepare 1 ¼ cup (100 g) of spinach by following the recipe on page 42.

3. Thinly slice ¾ of a cup (60 g) of shiitake mushrooms and 1 small onion, cut 1 small carrot into matchsticks. In a oiled frying pan, cook these ingredients separately, maintaining their crunchiness. Season with salt, pepper and set to the side.

4. Make *dalgyal-jidan* with 2 eggs (see p. 11).

5. In a saucepan, boil just under 1 cup (200 ml) of water with 2 tbsp (30 ml) of soy sauce, 1 tbsp (15 ml) of sesame oil and 2 tsp (10 ml) of sugar. Add the drained noodles and cook them over medium heat, stirring until the water has been completely absorbed. Turn off the heat and stir in the vegetables. Place the *dalgyal-jidan* on top and sprinkle with sesame seeds.

비빔국수

Bibim-guksu, cold noodles in a spicy sauce.

잔치국수

Janchi-guksu, thin noodles in a hot broth.

In a lot of Korean dishes toppings are freely chosen, so there is always a variety of colors. Place toppings on the thin wheat noodles, as cooked above. Add anchovy broth (see p. 37), then you will have janchi-guksu. If you don't use the broth, you can add cho-gochujang sauce (see p. 18) and your *bibim-guksu* is ready!

MANDUS, DUMPLINGS AND TTEOK, RICE CAKES

Mandus 만두, dumplings, can be filled in several different ways, with unusual ingredients or everyday ingredients like kimchi. They are served at special occasions as well as at street food stalls.

TTEOKMANDU-GUK, RICE CAKE SOUP 떡만둣국 WITH RICE CAKES AND DUMPLINGS

Beef or beef bone broth recipe (see p. 37). Options: with only rice cakes or dumplings. Or mix the two!

Let 14 oz (400 g) of coin-shaped rice cakes soak for 15 minutes in hot water. Put 12 *mandus* and the drained rice cakes in 1.5 quarts (liters) of beef broth and bring to a boil. Add 1 tsp (5 ml) of minced garlic, 1 tbsp (15 ml) of *cheong-jang* sauce. Cook for 3 to 5 minutes over medium heat. Turn off the heat, add 2 tbsp (30 ml) of chopped scallions and season with salt and pepper. Place a little *dalgyal-jidan* (see p. 11) and *gim-gui* flakes (see p. 44) on top.

4 types of dumplings

Pyeonsu

편수

Mimandu

미만두

Gaesungmandu

개성만두

Gyojamandu

교자

GAESUNG-MANDU, ROUND DUMPLING FILLED WITH MEAT

1   In a large bowl, mix 1 ¾ cups (220 g) of wheat flour and just under ¼ cup (20 g) of rice flour, pour in just over ¾ cup (190 ml) of warm water and knead to make a smooth dough. Let it rest for 1 hour, keeping it covered.

2   In a frying pan, cook ¾ cup (100 g) of chopped leeks on low heat with a little vegetable oil. Season with salt.

3   Prepare 1 ½ cups (250 g) of mung bean sprouts according to the recipe on page 42. Coarsely chop them.

4   In a bowl, mix 2 cloves of garlic, chopped, 2 pinches of garlic powder, 1 tbsp (15 ml) of soy sauce, 1 tbsp (15 ml) of sesame oil, 1 tbsp (15 ml) of rice wine. Add these ingredients to the ground meat, 3.5 oz (100 g) of beef and 3.5 oz (100 g) of pork, as well as 4.4 oz (125 g) of chopped firm tofu. Knead together. Stir in the vegetables and season with pepper.

5   Shape the dough into 25 balls, roll each one into a disk with a 3 inch (8 cm) diameter on floured surface.

6   Place a disk in your hand and put 1 tbsp (15 ml) of the filling in the middle. Moisten the edge of the disk with a little water, fold over to cover the filling and press to stick the edge down, then seal the two ends.

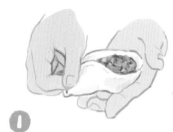

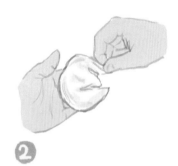

Tteok 떡 refers to cooked rice cakes and rice-based cakes. For salty dishes, they are made into cylinder-shaped batons called *garaetteok*.

떡볶이

떡볶이떡

떡국떡

가래떡

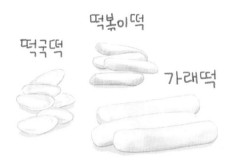

3 rice cake shapes for cooking (savory dishes): garaetteok, whole rice cakes; cut into slices for soup; small batons for toppoki.

Toppoki, rice cakes coated in a sweet, sour and spicy sauce.

꼭 먹어봐야 할 음식

SIGNATURE AND PARTY DISHES

Originally, in Korea, only special holidays were used as an opportunity to share a meal which included meat. Today, although meat has become more readily available, meat still marks a special occasion.

It's a chance for Koreans to get away from big cities to discover local areas and local restaurants famous for their regional specialties.

BiBIMBAP

Bibimbap 비빔밥, which means "mixed rice," is a balanced dish containing a carbohydrate, the rice, a variety of vegetables and a small amount of animal protein, either meat or eggs. There are many different types and everyone is free to express their creativity when making it. One of the theories behind the origin of bibimbap is the sharing of meals which comes from making offerings made to ancestors in Confucian culture.

Although *bibimbap* from Jeonju, the most well-known, has a sophisticated appearance with regards to representation of the five colors, other types are easier to make and use leftover *banchan* as toppings.

The choice of sauce, *gochujang* or soy sauce, is up to you.

BiBIMBAP FROM JEONJU 전주비빔밥

Jeonju is a town renowned for it gastronomy. Its *bibimbap* is often thought to be the most attractive.

1 Prepare 2 ¼ cups (450 g) of short grain rice using the recipe on page 31 and replace the water with bone broth.

2 Separate the whites from the yolks of 4 eggs. Season the whites with salt and cook them without browning in a frying pan over low heat, then cut into strips. Set the egg yolks to the side.

3 Prepare 1 cup (150 g) of soybean sprouts according to the recipe on page 42.

4 Thinly slice 1 cup (150 g) of shiitake mushrooms, cut 2 carrots and 2 cups (300 g) of zucchini into matchsticks. Heat a frying pan, pour in 2 tsp (10 ml) of oil and start by cooking the zucchini for 30 seconds with 2 tbsp (30 ml) of chopped scallions. Season with salt, pepper and set to the side. Cook the carrots in the same way (for 30 seconds), as well as the mushrooms (2 minutes). Set the vegetables to the side, in separate containers.

5 Cut 5.3 oz (150 g) of rump steak into thin slices, season with a third of the *bulgogi* sauce (see p. 46) and cook in a frying pan.

6 In 4 large bowls, place the rice, then each of the toppings, and 1 raw egg yolk in the middle. Garnish with pine nuts and ginkgo fruits. Serve the *gochujang* sauce and/or seasoned soy sauce (see p. 19) separately, everyone can then choose the sauce and quantity depending on what they like.

Sanchae bibimbap, vegetarian

A specialty from Gangwon province, this dish originally included only mountain vegetables, dried or freshly cut in the spring.

Today, all sorts of vegetables are used to make it: mushrooms, green vegetables, rehydrated zucchini slices, fern sprouts, platycodon roots and white radish with chili.

The crispy rice is prepared on the *dolsot*, an oiled and heated stone saucepan.

Seonggae bibimbap, with sea urchins from Geoje island

Made with sea urchins, seaweed flakes, young sprouts, sliced red cabbage and toasted sesame seeds.

Bibimbap from Andong

Andong is a city where many noble families originally came from. Toppings include platycodon roots, eggplant, spinach, beef preserved in soy sauce, soybean sprouts and toasted sesame seeds. It's served with seasoned soy sauce (see p. 19).

Bibimbap with bacon from Haeju in North Korea

Haeju is known for its bacon fried rice. It is topped with pork belly, chicken breast, fern sprouts, mung bean sprouts, water celery and toasted seaweed flakes. It is served with seasoned soy sauce.

There are many other less well-known types of *bibimbap*, made from regional produce.

산채비빔밥

성게비빔밥

안동비빔밥

해주비빔밥

탕류 CELEBRATION SOUPS

Although the "rice-soup" combination is the basis of daily meals, some soups act as the main dish, leaving the rice (although still important) as a secondary element. These are celebration soups, generously garnished, which are not necessarily accompanied by banchan but they do come with kimchi, as it's always included.

SEOLLEONGTANG, WHITE OX BONE BROTH 설렁탕

The rice can be served in the soup itself or on the side. *Kkaktugi kimchi* (see p. 60) goes perfectly with this dish.

1 Bring 2 quarts (liters) of bone and meat broth to the boil (see p. 37). Add 2 or 3 crushed cloves of garlic and season with salt and pepper.

2 Cook 3.5 oz (100 g) of thin wheat noodles, rinse with cold water and drain. Thinly slice the meat from the broth.

3 Put the noodles into 4 large bowls. Pour the hot broth into the bowls, add the sliced beef and sprinkle 1 tbsp (15 ml) of finely chopped scallions on top.

고사리

숙주

파

고추

소고기

육개장

Yukgaejang

Spicy beef broth, topped with beef, scallions, mung bean sprouts and fern sprouts. Served with chili oil on the side.

삼계탕

Samgyetang

This is a chicken (cockerel) soup garnished with medicinal herbs, the most famous being ginseng. The chicken (cockerel) is stuffed with sticky rice, jujube and garlic.

전 JEON, FRIED FOOD FOR PARTIES

Jeon 전 refers to deep-fried or pan-fried foods, coated in all-purpose flour and beaten egg. All sorts of ingredients can be prepared in this way: fish fillets, vegetables, meat, mushrooms, tofu, etc. Jeon is one of the signature dishes made for traditional holidays.

MODEUM-JEON, ASSORTED JEON 모둠 전

Beoseot-jeon
with shiitake mush-
rooms stuffed with
ground beef
버섯전

Sengsun-jeon
with white fish
생선전

Hobak-jeon
with zucchini
호박전

고추전
Gochu-jeon
with chilis stuffed
with ground beef

삼색전
Samsek-jeon
with mini beef
skewers, scallions,
pickled yellow
radish and surimi

두부전
Dubu-jeon
with tofu

1 Coat in flour.

2 Dip in beaten egg.

3 Pan-fry and garnish (optional) in an oiled pan.

해물파전

Jeon also includes filled pancakes. *Haemulpa-jeon* 해물파전, seafood and scallion pancake, this is a specialty from Busan, a port city. The scallions can be left whole for more of a crunch.

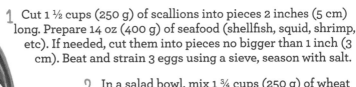

1 Cut 1 ½ cups (250 g) of scallions into pieces 2 inches (5 cm) long. Prepare 14 oz (400 g) of seafood (shellfish, squid, shrimp, etc). If needed, cut them into pieces no bigger than 1 inch (3 cm). Beat and strain 3 eggs using a sieve, season with salt.

2 In a salad bowl, mix 1 ¾ cups (250 g) of wheat flour with 1 ¼ cups (300 ml) of water, season with salt and pepper. Pour a quarter into another bowl, gently stir in a quarter of the scallions and a quarter of the seafood.

3 Heat a frying pan over medium heat, add a generous amount of oil, then pour the mixture into the pan, spreading it evenly. Baste with a quarter of the beaten eggs. Let it cook for 2 to 3 minutes, then flip the pancake over. Oil the pan again and continue to cook on this side for another 2 or 3 minutes.

4 Make another 3 pancakes in the same way. Serve hot with a vinegar-soy sauce (see p. 19).

빈대떡과 막걸리

Bindaetteok

Mung bean pancake, topped with mung bean sprouts, fern sprouts, kimchi and pork. Since the beginning of the 20th century, this dish has been a popular street food in Seoul, and it is still popular today. It goes very well with makkoli.

불고기: 직화 구이   BEEF

After a long period during which Buddhism was dominant, the Mongol invasion marked the introduction of meat to Korea, and with it, a large number of recipes for grilling directly on fire. In the past, animals were used to plow the fields and they were not slaughtered until the end of their lives, meaning that the meat was extremely tough. Marinating the meat in fermented sauces and fruit purées tenderized the meat. This explains the many sweet and sour marinade recipes in Korean cooking.

GRILLED BEEF

Bulgogi 불고기 is a grilled beef dish that is very popular among Koreans. There are many different regional recipes. The best types of bulgogi are prepared with hanwoo, a cattle breed native to Korea. Different types of grills are used: flat, domed with holes or cast-iron.

3 types of bulgogi

Seoul-style *bulgogi* is characterized by its sweet flavor and generous amounts of sauce. The sweet potato starch noodles can be dipped in this sauce.

서울식

언양식

Eonyang-style *bulgogi*: the meat is cut into strips and not ground.

광양식

Gwangyang-style *bulgogi*: charcoal, a specialty from this city, is used to grill the meat. Unlike other recipes, the meat is not marinated in advance, the sauce is added just before the meat is cooked.

SEOUL-STYLE BULGOGI RECIPE   갈비구이

1. Soak 1.7 oz (50 g) of *dangmyeon* noodles (see p. 68) in hot water for 30 minutes.

2. Thinly slice 14 oz (400 g) of sirloin steak. Wipe off the blood.

3. In a bowl, mix just under ½ a cup (100 ml) of soy sauce, ⅓ cup (80 ml) of honey, 3 cups (700 ml) of water, a purée made of ⅓ cup (50 g) of pear and ⅛ of a cup (25 g) of onion and 2 cloves of minced garlic. Season with pepper. Stir in the meat and let it marinate for 20 minutes.

4. Put the meat on the grill after letting any excess sauce drip off, pour the sauce into the grill pan and add ¾ cup (100 g) of *enoki* mushrooms, 1 chopped onion, ¾ cup (100 g) of chopped scallions and the drained noodles.

5. Cook for 3 to 6 minutes on high heat, to your liking.

6. Serve right away. Either eat it as is or wrap a bit of meat and a little rice in a salad leaf (see *ssam* p. 33).

Galbi-gui, grilled beef ribs   갈비 손질

Gui means "grilled" and *galbi* means "rib." This dish is as popular as *bulgogi*. Although they are seasoned in almost the same way, *galbi* is different due to its texture and particular flavor. This dish can also be braised, to make *galbi-jjim*.

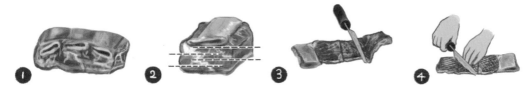

How to prepare the beef ribs
The rubbery membrane around the bone must be removed to ensure the meat has a tender texture. Precise cuts in the meat allow the seasoning to thoroughly penetrate the meat. The meat cooks quickly as it is not very thick, which is much better.

How should you cut the galbi?
Unlike bulgogi, galbi is cooked in large pieces and portioned out when served.

MARINATED BEEF AND DRIED BEEF

떡갈비

Tteok-galbi, marinated ground beef rib patties

The beef ribs are ground and mixed for a long time, which gives the meat both a tender and springy consistency. It is then combined with the *bulgogi* sauce and made into a patty, which is grilled in a frying pan or on a grill directly over a fire. This ground beef rib dish was initially meant for small children or elderly people who find it difficult to chew, but today, everyone eats it. It is delicious in a hamburger (see p. 111) with a little *kimchi*.

Yuk-hoe, steak tartare 육회

1. Cut 14 oz (400 g) of beef shin slices in the direction opposite to the muscle fibers, into strips 3 mm thick and 2 inches (5 cm) long. Wipe the blood off with a paper towel. Mix the meat with 1 tbsp (15 ml) of chopped scallions, 2 tsp (10 ml) of minced garlic, 1 tbsp (15 ml) of ground toasted sesame seeds, 2 tbsp (30 ml) of sugar, 4 tbsp (60 ml) of soy sauce and 1 ½ tbsp (22.5 ml) of sesame oil. Season with pepper.

2. Using a rolling pin, crush 1 ½ tbsp (22.5 ml) of pine nuts between two paper towels until you get a dry powder.

3. Cut 1 Asian pear into matchsticks. Thinly slice 1 clove of garlic.

4. Spread the pear on plates and place the slices of garlic and meat on top. Sprinkle on the pine nut powder.

5. If you want, you can add a raw egg yolk to each portion.

INGREDIENTS

Yukpo, dried beef

Koreans have a strong passion for dried foods; fish, vegetables, mushrooms and, in particular, beef. Making dried beef is a true art form. Combined with fruit, honey, soy sauce and sesame oil, it becomes almost like candy and goes well with an alcoholic drink.

Selection of dried beef.

PORK AND CHICKEN

돼지고기와 닭고기

Pork and chicken, meats that are more accessible than beef, are eaten during dinner with colleagues after work or, for students, with friends. Many small local restaurants offer delivery.

PORK   삼겹살구이

Samgyeopsal-gui, grilled pork belly and sides

This dish is symbolic of the post-war reconstruction period of the country. Rich, affordable, delicious, this dish sustained workers. It's also a very sociable dish, a little like raclette in France.

SIMPLIFIED RECIPE

1 Cut the pork belly, vegetables and fruits into thin strips. Place them in front of the guests with a variety of sauces (see p. 19) and grilling equipment. Everyone can create their *ssam* (see p. 33) by freely combining the meat with the other ingredients.

2 *Soju* 소주, sweet potato liquor, is almost essential to complete the meal.

Pyeonyuk, head cheese or pork, is eaten with a fermented shrimp sauce (see p. 19).

편육

SSam

Soju

쌈채소

나박김치

쌈장

삼겹살

파채

CHICKEN

Chimaek, fried chicken and beer

Fried chicken goes well with beer, which is why it's also known as *chimaek* 치맥, an abbreviation of *chikin-mekju* (chicken-beer). *Yangnyeom-chikin* is internationally known as: KFC (*Korean Fried Chicken*). What makes Korean fried chicken unique is that it is cooked in two stages, like fries. This dish is very popular among fans of Korean cooking.

치맥

치킨무

치킨쏘스

양념치킨
Yangnyeom-chikin, fried chicken with a sweet, sour and spicy sauce.

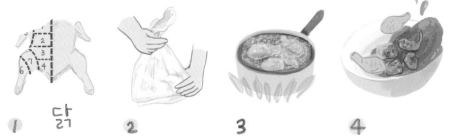

닭

1   **2**   **3**   **4**

1   Cut 3.3 lbs (1.5 kg) of chicken into 16 pieces. Let it marinate for 8 hours overnight in 1 ¼ cups (300 ml) of milk seasoned with salt and pepper.

2   Mix 2 cloves of minced garlic, ⅓ to ½ a cup (100-150 g) of *gochujang*, ⅓ cup (100 g) of ketchup, just over ⅓ cup (90 ml) of honey, 2 tsp (10 ml) of curry powder, 2 tbsp (30 ml) of soy sauce, 2 tsp (10 ml) of rice vinegar, 2 tbsp (30 ml) of toasted sesame oil and ½ cup (120 ml) of water. Season with pepper. Let it rest for 8 hours at room temperature.

3   Combine 1 ¼ cup (160 g) of Maïzena® (corn-flour) and all-purpose flour, and mix half of this with the chicken marinade.

4   Tip the remaining flour into a plastic bag, and then add the chicken. Seal it and shake it so that all the pieces of chicken are coated in flour.

5   Fry the chicken in oil at 338 °F (170 °C) for 3 to 6 minutes. Before eating, cook the chicken again for 1 to 3 minutes.

6   In a large saucepan, sauté just over ⅓ cup (50 g) of chopped carrots and just over ⅓ cup (50 g) of chopped onions for 20 seconds in a little oil, pour in the sauce and bring to the boil. Turn off the heat, stir in the fried chicken and mix well.

7   Sprinkle crushed peanuts on top and serve right away.

FISH 생선

These fish are mostly eaten dried or fermented. Koreans do not hesitate to travel long distances to eat fresh fish at port city restaurants. They are kept alive in tanks and butchered at the restaurant when guests request fish.

JOGIJJIM, FIVE COLOR STONE BASS

조기찜

굴비

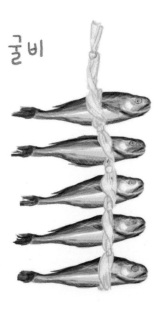

Youngwang gulbi: salt-cured and dried yellow stone bass, a Youngwang specialty, is a highly sought-after, luxury treat in Korea.

Steamed white fish, garnished with *gomyeong* (see p. 11); like vegetables or egg roll, this is both a party dish and a meal offering. It is light, delicate, healthy, in short, modern and yet one of the favorites of old-fashioned cooking.

1 Gut and scale 2 stone bass (sea bream or sea bass if you can't find any), weighing 14 oz (400 g) each. Make 3 incisions on each side. Season with salt, let them rest for 30 minutes and then pat dry.

2 Line a steamer basket with some scallions and then place the fish on top. Start cooking when a lot of steam is being released, at around 15 minutes.

3 Prepare some *dalgyal-jidan* (see p. 11). Grate the green part, the skin or close to the skin of ½ a cucumber and 6 dried jujubes (or carrots). Fry them separately, briefly, with a few drops of oil.

4 Arrange these *gomyeong*, decorative elements, nicely on the fish. Strands of dried chili can also be added. Serve hot with rice.

황태

Hwangtae

Whiting, a winter fish, is dried in the open air for several weeks in Gangwon province. The overnight freezing and thawing the next day breaks down the muscle fibers of the fish, making it appear crinkled so it absorbs the seasoning well and provides a pleasant texture.

Open-air fish drying farm in the snow.

눈 덮인 덕장

황태구이

Hwangtae grilled in a spicy sauce.

Eat raw

There are two ways of preparing raw fish: with or without a maturation period. Koreans tend to prefer matured fish, it has more of a bite, whereas fish that hasn't been matured is more melt-in-the-mouth. Chilled, sliced raw fish soup is very popular in the summer (see p. 95).

회

Hoe, raw fish dish with cho-gochujang sauce (see p. 19).

SHELLFISH

Koreans love shellfish, whether it is cooked, raw or fermented.

GAEJANG, CRAB SERVED RAW, MARINATED IN SOY SAUCE

게장

It is known as a "rice thief" because it's so tasty served with rice that your food will be gone before you realize.

The crab meat has a rich, umami taste - the fifth flavor, the flavor enhancer - this is an addictive dish that is prepared in the spring when the females are fat.

It's fun and delicious to eat the rice straight from the shell.

Some commonly eaten seafood in Korea

Moon snails

골뱅이

전복
Abalone

Sea pineapple

멍게

미더덕

Sea urchins

성게

Sea squirt

OJINGEO-SUNDAE, SQUID SAUSAGE

오징어순대

1 Stuff. 2 Seal with a skewer. 3 Cook. 4 Cut.

1 Separate the body and tentacles of 2 squid, each weighing 14 oz (400 g). Remove the innards from the body and rinse.

2 Stuffing: in an oiled frying pan, sauté just under 1 cup (120 g) of chopped *kimchi* (without liquid), just under 1 cup (120 g) of chopped onions and the chopped squid tentacles, until all liquid has evaporated. Stir in ¾ cup (150 g) of cooked sticky rice (see p. 31) and 10.5 oz (300 g) of chopped firm tofu. Season with salt and pepper.

3 Coat the inside of the squid bodies with flour, fill them with the stuffing, leaving a small space, then seal them using a skewer.

4 Let them steam for 2-3 minutes. Remove them and let them cool before cutting into slices.

Squid is one of the most popular seafoods in Korea. People like its elastic flesh. Dried and grilled squid is perfect as a snack or appetizer.

테마별 음식

COOKING BY CATEGORY

Food is an indicator of the different seasons and the natural environment. Learning about the cuisine and food customs of a country is one of the best ways of understanding its culture.

THE FOUR SEASONS

SPRING 봄

Spring is the season for harvesting bom-namul, spring greens, mountain vegetables (as mountains cover 70% of Korea) and meadow vegetables. Young sprouts are packed with vitamins. People go out to the country to harvest them, but also to get their bodies moving again after winter. An old folk song tells us that this was a wonderful occasion for young people to meet each other.

Young spring sprouts and edible flowers

배꽃

Pear flowers

두릅

Korean aralia sprouts

참나물

Pimpinella brachycarpa

쑥

Mugwort

곰취

Ligularia

유채꽃

Canola flowers

고사리

Fern sprouts

달래

Korean wild chives

냉이

Shepherd's purse

주꾸미

Jukkeumi, baby octopus in gochujang sauce: these baby octopus are fished from the sea off of the west coast. In Korea, these octopus are known for their invigorating properties.

두견주

Dugyoenju, azalea liquor: fragrant rice liquor with azalea flowers.

냉이나물

Nengii-namul, a cooked, shepherd's purse salad, a plant from the Brassicaceae family that appears in early spring and grows in France too.

For those that do not go to harvest, vegetable stalls offer a wide variety of fresh bom-namul.

화전과 쑥떡

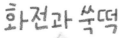

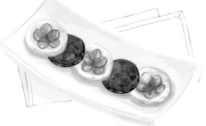

Jindallae-hwajeon, mini rice pancakes with azalea flowers and mugwort. They are eaten soaked in honey. Pear and canola flowers are also used.

SUMMER 여름

Summer in Korea is hot and humid, sweltering in some places. A huge amount of thirst-quenching foods are eaten, among which the unrivalled queen is watermelon.

Selection of local summer fruits and drinks: melon, grape, watermelon, misu-garu (grain powder used to make drinks).

Misu-garu, toasted barley milk with sugar, is highly nutritious and easy to drink, especially for those who have lost their appetite due to the heat.

Watermelon trucks.

Squeeze the grape, it will peel itself!
Korean grapes are easy to eat: gently squeeze them and the pulp will slide out into your mouth on its own.

KONG-GUKSU, SOY MILK NOODLES

1 Wash 1 ½ cups (200 g) of yellow soybeans and soak them overnight in 1 quart (liter) of water.

2 Drain them, then cook in a saucepan in 1 quart (liter) of water over high heat. Once it is boiling, let it simmer for another 10 minutes.

3 Drain and pour the cooked soybeans into a large bowl. While rinsing with cold water, rub the beans together with your fingers to remove the skins.

4 Blend the drained, de-skinned soybeans with 3 ⅓ cups (800 ml) of water until they are smooth and creamy. Strain through a sieve and only keep the thin liquid. Press to extract every drop. Season with a little salt and set to the side in a cool place.

5 For the cold noodles: cook 10.5 oz (300 g) of thin wheat noodles until tender, according to the method on page 69. Divide the noodles into 4 large bowls.

6 Add the soy milk and garnish with some cucumber, cut into matchsticks, and 1 slice of tomato. Serve chilled with salt on the side.

Ice cubes are often put in soups, which might seem a little strange, but with the heat of summer, you'll quickly get a taste for it!

평양냉면

Pyongyang naengmyeon, cold noodles from Pyongyang (see p. 69). Coming from a cold country, North Korea, this summer dish is loved by all Koreans, from both the North and the South; it's a symbol of a united Korea.

삼계탕

Samgyetang, ginseng chicken soup (see p. 77). Since ancient times, the health benefits of ginseng have been recognized worldwide. It was one of the first Korean products exported to the rest of the world on the silk road.

물회

Mulhoe, raw fish soup. Fish "swim" in a sweet and sour chilled soup, with doenjang (see p. 19) or chili powder.

AUTUMN 가을

After the fruity aroma of summer, the autumn table is filled with the smell of pine humus, taro and mushrooms. New rice, with its subtle but sweet flavor, relieves the memory of the intense summer heat. It's the season of harvest and plenty. The Moon, a reliable guide for farmers, is honored.

Songpyeon

This is a cake made from non-sticky rice, filled with cooked green soybeans, sugary sesame seeds, chestnuts or mung beans, cooked in a steamer basket lined with pine needles. It is delicious when paired with *sujeongwa*, a persimmon and cinnamon drink.

Songpyeon, moon cake, fragrant rice dough with pine leaves.

Chuseok, harvest festival: the whole family helps to make moon cakes.

삼

Ginseng

토란국

송이버섯

Songi beoseot,
matsutake mushrooms

토란

Taro soup with beef,
a special dish for chuseok

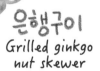

은행구이
Grilled ginkgo
nut skewer

수정과

Winter punch with
spices and persimmon
(see p. 120)

햅쌀

Hepssal,
new rice

겨울
WiNTER

Korean winter is white with frost and snow, and temperatures often drop to below 14 °F (-10 °C). This white color is also reflected in New Year's rice cake soup (see p. 70), which symbolizes a blank canvas to start the new year. The steam rising from street food is even more striking in the cold air.

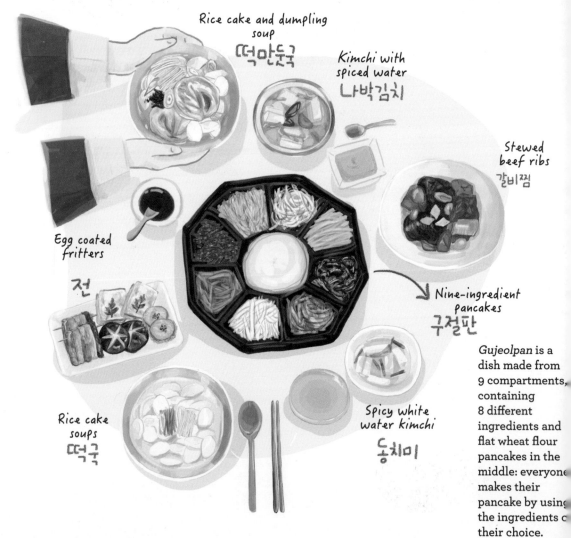

Rice cake and dumpling soup
떡만둣국

Kimchi with spiced water
나박김치

Stewed beef ribs
갈비찜

Egg coated fritters
전

Nine-ingredient pancakes
구절판

Rice cake soups
떡국

Spicy white water kimchi
동치미

Gujeolpan is a dish made from 9 compartments, containing 8 different ingredients and flat wheat flour pancakes in the middle: everyone makes their pancake by using the ingredients of their choice.

Sechan 세찬, New Year's meal
Dumplings, which used to be a luxurious treat (but nowadays are very common), are made for special occasions like New Year's.

김장 김치 · 수육

New Kimchi tray: new kimchi, oysters, boiled pork

At the start of winter, making winter *kimchi*, *kimjang*, is an important annual activity. The hostess offers the participants a simple snack to renew their strength, made from *kimchi*, pork, *soju* oysters and white liquor.

To eat, you make your own appetizer, with a little *kimchi* and a piece of pork with or without oysters.

동지 팥죽

Patjuk, kidney bean soup with rice cake balls and dongchimi, white radish water kimchi

A dish which protects against dark spirits, it is eaten during the winter solstice, the longest night of the year. Evil spirits were thought to be afraid of the color red, so the soup was splashed on the corners of houses.

동치미

See p. 61

See p. 61

Comforting street food: warming sweet treats to eat on the go

호빵

Hopang, steamed filled buns

Hotteok, pancake filled with brown sugar syrup (see p. 107)

(see p. 107)

군고구마

Gun-goguma, baked sweet potato

POPULAR FAMILY TRADITIONS

Family is at the heart of Korean life. Influenced by Confucian philosophy, family traditions are very important and food acts as a symbol of spiritual and material well-being. The colorful appearance of dishes and decorations is based on the belief in obangsaek (see p. 10).

IBAJi EUMSIK WEDDINGS 이바지 음식

결혼식

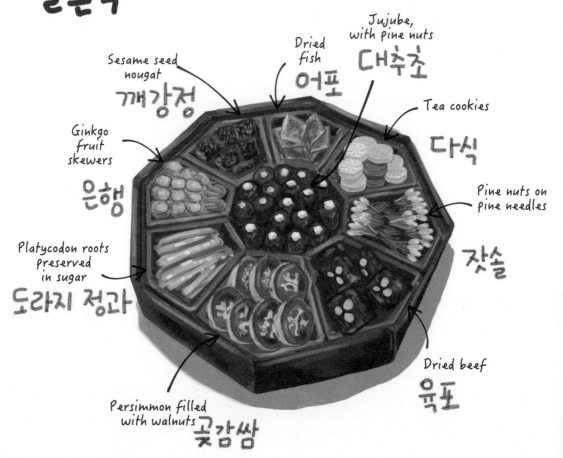

Sesame seed nougat
깨강정

Dried fish
어포

Jujube, with pine nuts
대추초

Tea cookies
다식

Ginkgo fruit skewers
은행

Pine nuts on pine needles
잣솔

Platycodon roots preserved in sugar
도라지 정과

Persimmon filled with walnuts 곶감쌈

Dried beef
육포

PEBAEK: CEREMONY TO GREET THE IN-LAWS

폐백

Today, wedding ceremonies are conducted in a western format. However, *pebaek* — the first time the groom's parents are greeted, a Korean tradition — involves sharing alcoholic drinks, "receiving jujubes," symbolizing the promise of children, and wishing the couple well. The food on the table, *Ibaji eumsik*, is provided by the bride's family. It is often dried or preserved.

생일 BIRTHDAYS

In North America, birthdays are celebrated each year with the same amount of enthusiasm (although the ten's are celebrated a little more), but in Korea, birthdays at the start of life (100th day after birth and at 1 year old) and later in life (at 60 or 70) are properly celebrated with party dishes and presents.

Food for a 1ˢᵗ birthday

돌상

Rice cake, baeksulgi: clarity, cleanliness, long life

5-colored rice cake, osek-songpyeon: harmony

Kidney bean rice cakes, susu-kyungdan: to ward off evil spirits

Noodles: long life

Jujubes: promise of children

Rice: wealth

Dishes for other birthdays are fairly simple, seaweed or 'long' noodle soup, symbolic of long life. Today, the western tradition of "cake" has become an essential component.

Table of objects for a 1ˢᵗ birthday

환갑

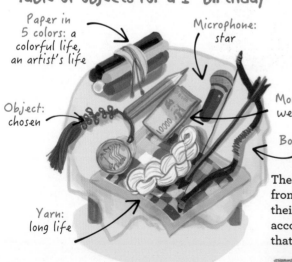

Paper in 5 colors: a colorful life, an artist's life

Microphone: star

Object: chosen

Money: wealth

Bow and arrow: bravery

Yarn: long life

The table is placed in front of the baby and their future is predicted according to the object that they pick.

60ᵗʰ birthday meal
The food, including desserts, candy or fruits, shows the lavishness of the party.

DEATH AND
OFFERINGS TO ANCESTORS

There is a unique culture of respect for the elderly and ancestors.

uneral food

During funerals, food is provided for guests. Although here are no strict rules, *yukgaejang* soup (see p. 77), spicy eef soup, is the most commonly served dish. Nowadays, ea or small gifts of thanks have replaced food.

장례 음식

제사상

Food offering

Serving ancestors is as important as serving living relatives. There are many customs with strict rules. This is still the case today, although the preparation is becoming less complicated.

Fruits are cut into to allow their fragrant smell to spread, because it was believed that souls were sustained by aromas.

Fish is not allowed as it drives ghosts away, including those of ancestors.

1–9: Rice, cakes, broths, alcohol
10–14: Meat and fish
15–17: Meat, vegetables and fish in soup
18–22: Dried fish, namul (leafy greens),
vegetables and fermented sauces
23–28: Fruits and desserts

사찰 음식 SACHAL EUMSIK, TEMPLE FOOD

Buddhism ruled Korea for 1,200 years, leaving behind a legacy of vegetarianism and a philosophy of frugality. Although there is more and more of a trend towards eating meat in modern food, vegetarian recipes are still very important in Korea. Today, temples open their doors to all who want to learn about temple food and they are attracting more and more people.

Buddhist meals in public restaurants

Preserved burdock root

Deodok (codonopsis lanceolata) root salad with a spicy dressing

Pickled lotus flower root

Fried tofu with vegetables, sweet and sour sauce

Vegetable and flower pancake with sauce

Mung bean jelly and spring vegetable soup

The dishes are more complex and varied compared to those in temples.

© Cultural Corps of Korean Buddhism

KIMBUGAK, FRIED DRY SEAWEED COATED IN 부각 STICKY RICE

1. Cover one gim seaweed sheet with cooked sticky rice, 1 tbsp (15 ml) for one sheet. Let this dry. Cut into 1.5 inch (4 cm) squares while it is still flexible, then let it dry completely.

2. Heat the frying oil to 356 °F (180 °C). Fry the seaweed for around twenty seconds. Season with salt.

Tradition: reflections before the meal
Where has this food come from?
Do I deserve it?
I give thanks for the farmers who produced it.
I accept this meal to maintain the good health
of my body in order to be granted wisdom.

발우공양

Lotus flower tea

This is served in a large bowl with a whole lotus flower in the tea. The lotus, a Buddhist symbol, is eaten in many different ways: its flower and leaves in teas, its dried seeds as dried fruits, its root as a vegetable.

연꽃잎차

길거리 음식

STREET FOOD

Children, teenagers, older people, office workers in a rush... everyone has a reason to go and eat a quick, exotic, fun or affordable snack.

Some street food dishes

계란빵
Egg bread

떡볶이
Toppoki

핫도그
Korean-style corn dog

회오리감자
Tornado (curly) fries

순대
Black pudding

HOTTEOK, PANCAKE FILLED WITH BROWN SUGAR SYRUP

1. In a large bowl, mix ⅓ cup (75 g) of muscovado sugar, just under ¼ cup (15 g) of ground, roasted peanuts and ½ to 1 tsp (2.5-5 ml) of cinnamon powder. Set this to the side.

2. In a salad bowl, add 1 ½ cups (200 g) of T55 wheat flour and just under ⅓ cup (40 g) of glutinous (sticky) rice flour, then add the activated yeast mixed into 1 ½ tbsp (22.5 ml) of water, and just under ¾ cup (170 ml) of warm water. Knead the mixture — the dough is very sticky! Let it rise, covered, in a warm place.

3. When it has doubled in size, heat a saucepan over low heat. Generously coat the pan and your hands in oil.

4. Take an egg-sized piece of dough and form into a ball, place it in the palm of your hand, flatten to make a dip in the middle and fill with 1 tbsp (15 ml) of the filling. Pull and bring the dough together to seal the filling inside. Cook in the pan for 30 seconds, then flip and flatten it with a spatula. Continue to cook for another 2 or 3 minutes, until the pancake is nicely browned. Serve right away.

호떡

북한요리 NORTH KOREAN SPECIALTIES

Despite the divide, the two Korea's have the same culinary heritage. South Koreans are extremely interested in North Korean food. Restaurants specializing in North Korean food, run by refugees, are very popular.

PYONGYANG NAENGMYEON, COLD NOODLES FROM PYONGYANG

A winter specialty, originally from Pyongyang, it is now a popular summer dish in the South. Many people who call themselves foodies are able to appreciate the broth, a delicate flavor for some, but a little too bland for others.

Recipe

1 Mix together 3 ¼ cups (750 ml) of beef broth (see p. 37) and 3 ¼ (750 ml) of *dongchimi* water (see p. 61). Season with *cheongjang* sauce and salt. Set this to the side in a cool place.

2 Thinly slice the meat from the broth. Cut 2 hard-boiled eggs in half. Thinly slice 1 ½ cups (200 g) of cucumber and 1 cup (150 g) of *dongchimi*.

3 Cook 8.5 oz (240 g) of *nengmyeon* buckwheat noodles, rinse thoroughly with cold water.

4 Split the noodles between 4 large bowls, pour in the broth and add the toppings. Serve with vinegar and mustard on the side for those who want to add a more punchy flavor.

Nongma-guksu, cold potato starch noodles from Hamhung.

냉면

Pyongyang naengmyeon

아바이순대

Abai-sundae, blood sausage with rice and vegetables: a specialty from Abai-maeul, village for North Korean refuge.

NORTHERN KIMCHI VS SOUTHERN KIMCHI

Southern *kimchi* is more richly garnished and more ed in color (thanks to the chili!).

ince the end of the war, the North has been a closed ountry; due to this, in some ways, its food has etained certain pre-war elements.

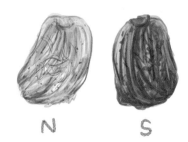

N   S

FOOD FROM GAESUNG 개성요리

he city of Gaesung, capital during the Goryeo dynasty, is famous for its refined ood. Some recipes are still made today, even in the South.

보쌈김치

Bossam kimchi:
Pe-tsaï cabbage
kimchi surprise

개성약과

Gaesung-yakgwa:
Spiced puff pastry

편수

면조말이구이

urkey roll-up

 new food trend in North Korea that started a ew years ago. Turkey, which is easy to breed, as become a very popular meat.

Gaesung-pyeonsu:
square dumplings

외래 음식 DISHES FROM OTHER COUNTRIES

Some Korean dishes were inspired by recipes from other countries.

JJAJANG-MYEON 짜장면

Noodles in black bean sauce, this dish was introduced by the Chinese community in Korea at the start of the 20th century. This is one of the most popular dishes among Koreans, especially children.

Jjampong: this spiced seafood noodle soup is originally a Chinese dish and was introduced to Korea via Japan.

춘장

Black bean paste

Yellow radish
단무지

Steak tartare

This recipe goes back to the 13th century, the period where Gengis Khan's empire spread the idea of consuming raw beef to the West and even to the East, including Korea. The taste of sesame oil and sweetness of pear make it different from the French recipe (see p. 82).

잡채고로케

Japchae goroke, croquettes filled with noodles and vegetables

Goroke are originally from Belgium; they're like croquettes. After having been adapted in Japan, the recipe further evolved in Korea with the addition of a new filling, *japchae* (see p. 69).

부대찌개

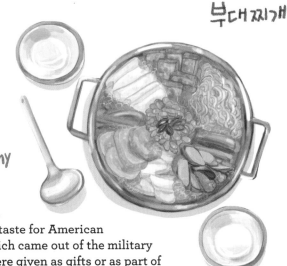

Budae jjigae, army stew

During the war, Koreans developed a taste for American products which came out of the military bases and were given as gifts or as part of trades. The cooked meats in the spiced broth gives a delicious flavor.

라면

Ramyeon, instant noodles

The noodles were originally made with flour delivered by American humanitarian aid and using a Japanese recipe to help rejuvenate Koreans after the war. They are still popular today, with the addition of new flavors.

불고기버거

치즈떡볶이

Cheese toppoki

Cheese was only recently introduced in Korea and it quickly won over young people thanks to its smooth, rich taste.

Bulgogi hamburger

The famous American food has been adapted using *bulgogi* steak (see p. 82).

LUCKY FOODS

Academic success is a guarantee of social success in Korea. For this reason, university entrance exams are crucial. Their importance has generated irrational beliefs giving certain foods all sorts of symbolic meanings.

FOODS TO AVOID

수능 금기 음식

Seaweed soup, unsafe soup: generally recommended for its excellent digestibility and nutritious benefits, it should be avoided during exam periods due to its slippery texture (a trip hazard), just like bananas.

Fried egg or bread with a shape similar to the number zero would bring bad luck (a bad grade).

LUCKY FOODS

Nougat box

When an exam date is approaching, it's customary to give good-luck gifts. The most popular choices are nougats and sticky rice balls.

엿

RICE NOUGAT RECIPE

In a saucepan, reduce the rice syrup over low heat while stirring. When the syrup reaches a thick consistency, stir in the dried fruits (sesame, peanuts, etc.). Pour it onto a base of soybean or potato starch powder and then cover the top with powder. Cut it into small pieces with a knife while dusting with powder to prevent sticking. Keep in a cool place.

Sticky rice balls:
to help get a better handle
on different challenges,
thanks to the sticky power
of the rice.

A new, more rational trend:
chocolates, which provide energy.

찹쌀떡

다과와 음료

DESSERTS AND DRINKS

In the past, alcohol and candy were part of Korean customs and played a part in many different traditions.

The refined and colorful appearance of the candy links it to spiritual symbols during these ceremonies and family events.

Today, the "western" dessert culture has aroused the foodie curiosity in Koreans, who have been quick to adopt this dessert culture.

TTEOK, RICE CAKES, AND GWAJUL, DESSERTS

Although the notion of dessert itself does not exist in Korean culture, there are many delicious treats that go with tea or alcohol. The main ingredients are rice, legumes and vegetables, not just fruits, but also root vegetables, for example, preserved radish, platycodon or lotus. Traditionally, wheat was rarely used.

TTEOK, RICE CAKES
떡

백설기
Baekseolgi: shortbread-like rice cake.

시루떡
Siru-tteok: shortbread-like cake with kidney beans.

절편
Jeolpyeon: spongy rice cake with mugwort.

영양떡
Young-yang-tteok: soft rice cake with soybeans and chestnuts.

증편
Jeungpyeon: soft rice cake with makko (rice beer)

오색경단
Osek-kyungdan: sticky rice balls coated in different colored powders.

약식
Yaksik: spiced rice with dried fruits.

인절미
Injeolmi: sticky rice cake coated in roasted soybean powder.

개성주악
Gaesung-juak: fried sticky rice cake soaked in rice syrup.

1 In a glass bowl, mix 2 ¼ cups (300 g) of glutinous rice flour with 1 ⅓ cups (320 ml) of hot water, adding 2 pinches of salt. Cook for 6 minutes in a microwave, keeping it covered. Stir the dough and put it back in the microwave for another 6 minutes. After this, the dough should be translucent. Let it cool for a few minutes.

2 Spread 10 tbsp (150 ml) of roasted soybean powder on a cutting board. Put the dough on the board using a wet spatula. Cut into 2 inch (4 cm) squares ½ an inch (1.5 cm) thick while dusting the dough and knife with more powder to prevent sticking.

GWAJUL, DESSERTS 과줄

타래과
Taraegwa: ginseng or ginger fried, wheat dough cookies.

유과
Yugwa: puffed sticky rice cake with rice syrup.

약과
Yakgwa: spiced wheat puff pastry and honey.

다식
Dasik: bite-sized pastries colored with powders, to be served with tea.

율란
Yullan: chestnut dough with pine nuts.

곶감쌈
Gotgamssam: dried persimmon filled with walnuts.

모과편 / 오미자편
Omija-pyeon and mogwa-pyeon: omija jelly and quince.

유자단자
Yuja-danja: mung bean cake with yuzu (see p. 17).

배오미자 정과
Bae-omija-jeongwa: pear preserved in omija juice.

Gotgamssam 곶감쌈 recipe, walnuts wrapped in dried persimmon

Open the dried persimmon (preferably semi-dried) by cutting the fruit lengthways. Roll it back up tightly around a shelled walnut. Set it to the side to firm up. Cut into slices when ready to eat.

HWACHAE AND BINGSU

Hwa, means "flower." These colorful, slightly sharp and refreshing sweet punches are enjoyed cold in the summer and hot in the winter.

YUJA-HWACHAE, FRUIT AND YUZU JUICE PUNCH

유자화채

1 In a large bowl, mix the chopped flesh of 1 or 2 yuzu fruits and ¼ cup (60 g) of sugar.

2 Cut the peel into thin strips. Peel 1 Asian pear and cut into matchsticks 2 mm thick. Deseed ½ a pomegranate and stir into the *yuzu* mixture. Pour in 2 ½ cups (600 ml) of cold water and stir. Sprinkle in a few pine nuts. Serve cold.

유자단지

YUJA-DANJI, PUNCH WITH PRESERVED, STUFFED YUZU

A very sophisticated dessert. The citrus fruit is filled with a mixture of raw chestnuts, dried jujube and black mushrooms, all very finely grated, and then preserved for several days in syrup. It is consumed once water is added.

Baesuk:
Ginger-poached pear,
with peppercorns.

배숙

BINGSU, CRUSHED ICE WITH DIFFERENT TOPPINGS

빙수

A must-have summer treat. There are endless flavor combinations, but the principle is the same for each one made. Crush ice or frozen milk cubes. Add a fruit syrup or condensed milk. Sprinkle fresh or candied fruit, or even rice cakes, candied beans, cookies, chocolate shavings, etc. on top.

Most popular ingredients

Injeolmi rice cake (see p. 117)

인절미

Roasted soybean powder

→ 콩가루

Watermelon

Mango

Strawberries

Cookies or chocolate shavings

Sweet kidney bean paste

단팥

전통 음료 SOFT DRINKS

The drinks can be consumed with or without sugar. Traditionally, they have a medicinal use. In the past, honey provided the sweet taste, but today, it is often replaced with sugar.

Omija-hwachae, omija berry punch

오미자화채

Omija berry

Azalea flower and/or pear

+ SUGAR

1   2   3

Omija berries are often used in drinks due to their pretty red color and their sweet yet sharp and astringent taste. For more sweetness, let the dried berries infuse overnight in cold water.

Sujeongwa, spiced persimmon winter punch

A cold drink to be enjoyed in the winter.

1. Infuse just over ½ cup (60 g) of chopped ginger and 2.1 oz (60 g) of cinnamon sticks, separately, each in 1.2 quarts (liters) of water over medium heat for 30 minutes, keeping both covered.

2. Strain and combine the two in a saucepan, add just under ¼ cup (35 g) of brown sugar and just over ¼ cup (65 g) of white sugar and boil for another 10 minutes with the lid on. Let this cool and then stir in 1 to 1 ½ (200-250 g) of semi-dried persimmon. Place this in the refrigerator until the persimmon is tender.

3. Serve cold, leaving the persimmon and garnish with some pine nuts.

수정과 Sujeongwa

FERMENTED SOFT DRINKS

모과차

Mogwa-cheong, fermented quince syrup

Cheong, fermented syrup, is used for infusions and sweet and salty recipes. This way of "raw" preserving better retains the flavor of the product used. *Maesil-cheong* ("plum syrup") and *sengang-cheong* ("ginger syrup") are prepared in the same way.

Nuruk

Gamju, sweet rice punch fermented with nuruk (starter): a drink made from rice alcohol (see p. 125) with a short fermentation period. It's a fizzy, naturally sweet drink. It has a very slight alcohol content, so children can still drink it.

Cheong recipe

1 In a bowl, soften 1 ½ cups (200 g) of grated quince flesh in just over ½ cup (200 g) of acacia honey. Pour this into a 17 oz (500 ml) jar, then seal it.

2 Let it ferment for 1 month at room temperature, stirring every 2 days (only for the first month). Continue to preserve for another 2 months as is or just the syrup on its own after straining.

3 Mix the *cheong* with some hot water. You can alter the amount to your liking.

4 *Cheong* can be stored for several months

Malt (dried barley sprouts): thanks to the amylase in the barley sprout, the rice produces a sweet and milky drink, sikhye, which looks similar to gamju.

차 TEAS AND INFUSIONS

The tea is fundamentally linked to the Buddhist spirit. The subtle flavor o
the green leaves is enjoyed in tranquility. Among the tea leaves used
is nokcha, green tea, the most commonly used.

DAGU, TEA SERVICE 다구

찻잔
Tchatjan:
tea cups

차통
Tchatong:
tea pot

다관
Dagwan:
teapot

개반
Gaeban:
lid-holder

숙우 Sukwu:
a large bowl "controls"
the temperature of the
tea before it is served i
individual cups.

There are three types of tea leaves

녹차
Tea leaves

감잎차
Persimmon
leaves

콩잎차
Soybean leaves

MEDICINAL INFUSIONS

rinking infusions really is one of the
est health practices. Many medicinal
lants, berries, flowers and roots are used,
ncluding the famous ginseng. There are
pecial tea rooms for these types of teas,
ometimes also offering health tips.

국화차

구기자차

Chrysanthemum
flower tea

Goji berry tea

EVERYDAY TEAS

eas are enjoyed throughout the day.
he most common are roasted grain
r roasted rice teas.

Store-bought bottled teas and
infusions:
in convenience stores, there is a
wide selection of mass-produced,
unsweetened drinks available.

수늉

보리차

ung-ngeung, roasted rice tea

After cooking the rice in a saucepan, you
can remove the roasted rice stuck to the
bottom and dry it, or pour water directly
on it.

Boil it in a large amount of water until you
have a semi-milky liquid. The tea is enjoyed
at the end of the meal. The roasted rice
grains are eaten with it.

Boricha, roasted barley tea

1 Rinse and drain the barley. In a frying pan
over high heat, dry them out for 1 minute
while stirring, then lower the heat and toast
them, still stirring, until browned. Let cool.

2 Bring 1 quart (liter) of water with 4 tbsp
(60 ml) of roasted barley to a boil, with
the lid on, then lower the heat and let boil
for another 10 to 15 minutes. Drink the tea
either hot or cold.

술 ALCOHOL

Koreans' love of fermentation does not exclude alcohol. Wealthy families kept their own recipes, just like kimchi. Even though the most popular alcohols are beer, soju, makolli and cocktails including these ingredients, these forgotten traditional recipes are also making a come-back.

NURUK

The starter is what gives this alcohol its taste.

In Korea, traditional alcohols are mostly made from cereals. Alcoholic fermentation of cereals starts with making the *nuruk*, Korean starter. It is made with mung beans, wheat, sorghum, millet, barley or rice.

Then the rice is fermented with the starter, after which it is filtered, producing a milky liquid, *makkoli*, titrated at around 7°, which is fizzy with a more or less mild taste.

If it is left to mature for longer, around 100 days, the liquid will become clear, *yak-ju*, a luxury alcohol, titrated at 13° to 16°.

Rice

Wheat

15 days

NURUK 누룩

30 days

Rice pasta

water

cooked rice

2-3 days

30°C

100 days

4-14 days

Bamboo colander

Ihwaju 이화주

Yak-ju 약주

Makkoli 막걸리

Alcohol to eat by spoon

Making Korean alcohol

1 Making *nuruk* (starter)

2 Mix the rice with the rehydrated *nuruk*

3 Put in a jar and add water

4 Fermentation (a long period to get clear alcohol)

5 Filtering

TALGI-JU, STRAWBERRY SOJU INFUSION, SIMPLE SOJU RECIPE

1 Cut into 3 cups (500 g) of strawberries in 2 or 3 places, put them in a large jar with ¾ cup (150 g) sugar, layering the two ingredients, close and let the sugar dissolve for one day.

2 Pour in 1 quart (liter) of *soju* (minimum 25°) and seal. Let it infuse for 2 weeks in a dark place.

3 Strain the strawberries using a sieve, then finely strain the liquid using a coffee filter. Pour the alcohol produced into a bottle, seal and let it mature for 1 month.

딸기주

Ttalgi-ju, strawberry ju infusion.

Juan-sang, a table prepared to serve alcohol.

Traditional *soju* is made by distilling *yak-ju*.

주

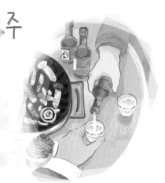

Mass-produced soju.

Nowadays, the name soju often refers to the factory-made product, created by diluting the ethanol from fermentation. It is affordable and popular.

Hand-made soju

오미자와인

Fruit maceration

Fruit can be macerated during fermentation or it can be added to the finished alcohol product. The most well-known are *bokbunja*, Korean raspberry, *moeru*, mountain grapes, or *maesil*, plum.

Fruit wines 100% fruit alcohols — peach, persimmon, apple or omija, etc. —, new for Koreans, are increasingly popular among young people.

INDEX

As an end to this book, I would like to express my gratitude to Aurélie, my editor at Mango. Huge thanks to AhnJi for her illustrations, which brought this book to life. I would also like to thank Brigitte and Steve for their brilliant advice, and not forgetting Jun, who has supported me throughout this project.

Luna Kyung

I would particularly like to thank Aurélie and Sylvaine for having made this project, which I am delighted to share with my readers, possible. A huge thanks to Luna, for having given me the opportunity to be involved in this wonderful project. Thanks to my sister Hyo-Eun for designing the Korean title, and to my parents and friends, who were the inspiration for the characters in this book.

AhnJi

A FIREFLY BOOK

Published by Firefly Books Ltd. 2022
First published in French by Mango, Paris, France — 2021
© Mango, Paris, 2021
Text © Luna Kyung
Illustrations © AhnJi

First printing

Library of Congress Control Number: 2022932284

Library and Archives Canada Cataloguing in Publication
Title: Korean cuisine : an illustrated guide / written by Luna Kyung ; illustrated by Ahnji.
Other titles: Cuisine coréenne illustrée. English
Names: Kyung, Luna, author. | Ahnji, illustrator.
Description: Translation of: La cuisine coréenne illustrée. | Includes index. | Includes some text in Korean.
Identifiers: Canadiana 2022017010X | ISBN 9780228103899 (softcover)
Subjects: LCSH: Cooking, Korean. | LCGFT: Cookbooks.
Classification: LCC TX724.5.K65 K9813 2022 | DDC 641.59519—dc23

Published in Canada by
Firefly Books Ltd.
50 Staples Avenue, Unit 1
Richmond Hill, Ontario
L4B 0A7

Published in the United States by
Firefly Books (U.S.) Inc.
P.O. Box 1338, Ellicott Station
Buffalo, New York
14205

Art management: Sylvaine Beck
Page layout: Studio Blick
Translator: Travod International Ltd.

Printed in China